The Magic of Mayfair

by

Jason T. Shapiro

Cover and page design by Peter Weisz Publishing
www.peterweisz.com

Published by **TREE MOUTH Books**
　　　　treemouthbooks@gmail.com

Shapiro, Jason T., November 2019
　　　　The Magic of Mayfair / Jason T. Shapiro
　　　　Memoir — Biography — Nostalgia — Self-Help — Personal Improvement

ISBN: 978-0-359-97984-4

Printed in the United States of America by Lulu.com.
1 2 3 4 5 6 7 8 9 10

To Andrea:

Thank you for all your love and support
throughout the journey of writing this book.

To Alyssa and Ryan:
Dream the biggest dreams.
Anything is possible!

I Love You!

Table of Contents

Author's Foreword

I have always believed that the essence of our life is found somewhere between the past and the present. There is a crossroad in time that defines who we were, who we are, and who we will become.

In 2017, I decided to embark on a journey to write a book. Crazy, I know. This wasn't just going to be any book, mind you. I was going to actually attempt to outline the crossroads of my own life and map out exactly how I became the person I am today… Who I was, who I am, and who I will become. I was going to literally reach into my soul, let the words flow from my fingertips, and see what would happen.

It ended up becoming one of the most life changing moments I have ever experienced. Exposing your own personal truth is powerful, painful, and also extremely liberating. Then immortalizing that truth within the pages of a book for the world to read is just honestly frightening. Going to a place of complete vulnerability wasn't easy and at times extremely uncomfortable. However, I have found that self-awareness is the road to self-acceptance.

So, how was I going to begin this story? Well, for most of my adult life I have memorialized my childhood. Why, you might ask? For me, it was a time of pure simplicity, innocence, and joy. My life was filled with people that I loved. Family, friends, and then something else very important in this story… A place. Somewhere so special, that it not only became the title of this book, but the backdrop of my life. This was a place where happiness and magic radiated through the air. I was very fortunate to call Mayfair Court in Clearwater, Florida my childhood home.

The next part of the story would be the task of layering in all those people that meant so much to me. Taking the memories that I had preserved in my mind for decades and then bringing those individuals back to life. Capturing the core of who they were and how they impacted my life was critical. I worked hard to ensure the words that I wrote represented their truth. Each person had their distinct characteristics and personalities that left a lasting impression on me to this very day.

How would I select the stories that I would tell? Well, that part kind of just happened as my fingers hit the keys. Nothing was predetermined, or sketched out. I simply would expand on a memory I had, or a story I was told. With each stroke on the keyboard, I slowly started to see the crossroads of my life appear before my eyes. A map of how I became the person I am today. I had created the blueprint of me.

Lastly, I wanted to share something very unique and special about this book. I was always fascinated with the concept of off-screen narrating. Being that I truly wanted this book to feel like you were watching a movie, it was something I decided to incorporate into this story. What if I was able to pop in and provide context on how I viewed my past, but in the present time? It added an additional layer of emotion and authenticity that I am very proud of.

Thank you for allowing me to take you on this adventure. Now it's time for you to experience…

THE MAGIC OF MAYFAIR!

Every house has a secret and every street has a story.

Chapter One

The Magic Begins

Summer of 1983

Our childhood is a distant reminder that absolute innocence and joy exists in its purest form. A road if traveled back, will take us to a place where time stands still and memories of before will surface through our souls.

The blinding rays of the warm summer sun radiate through the air. It's a glorious day!

Eight-year-old Jason Shapiro, nicknamed Toad by his father, is swimming underwater in an outdoor screened-in pool.

He is wearing swim goggles and nose plugs while his mushroom-shaped hair flows gracefully like seaweed atop the ocean. There is pure silence.

Jason begins to gradually surface and swims towards the edge. Suddenly, he pops out of the water like a jack-in-the-box filled with excitement!

He briskly exits the pool, shuffles across the hot Chattahoochee patio deck, and grabs his HE-MAN backpack. Jason takes his towel out and quickly attempts to dry off.

Still dripping with water, he walks over to the opened sliding glass door. Cautiously, Jason creeps into his beautiful new house that is still under construction.

The roaring sound of power saws and drills can be heard coming from the bedrooms located next to the pool.

Larry Shapiro is wearing his standard uniform—pleated khaki pants, a polo shirt (tucked into his underwear), and dress shoes. He's talking to the general contractor, with both arms animated, gesturing in the air. Larry has enough energy to run a marathon…Twice!

NOTE: *This is Jason in the present day. I am the eight-year-old boy that you have met in this story. When you see text inside a box like this, you'll know that it is me speaking to you in the current time. I will be popping in every so often to set the scene and provide context on what you have just read. Kind of like the off-screen narrator.*

Annnd… That's my father, Lawrence Shapiro! Let's just say it was "Larry's World" and we were all living in it. Even though our house was only about 75 percent built, my dad thought it was a good idea to have me go swimming in a live construction zone while he did an unscheduled "check-in" with the general contractor.

Multiple construction workers are seen in action cutting floor tiles, sawing baseboards, and painting the newly constructed walls.

"TOAD! Grab your bag and towel! IT'S TIME TO GO!" Larry shouts so fiercely that it startles the workers.

Jason and Larry begin to make their way toward the front door.

On his way out, Larry accidentally knocks over two opened paint cans that are sitting on the floor.

He yells over to the painter, "Hey, sorry, Mark!" (Although the painter is clearly wearing a t-shirt that is embroidered with the name Paul).

The painter shakes his head in annoyance and gives Larry the middle finger once his back is turned.

Larry continues marching through the house and then *finally* exits through the front door. Desperately, Jason tries to keep up with his father as he leaves a large trail of pool water throughout the freshly laid tile floors.

They both shuffle down the crowded driveway filled with construction trucks and painting vans.

Jason looks up at his father, pulls off his nose plugs, and innocently questions, "Dad, were we allowed to stop by today? It doesn't even look like the house is ready to move into yet."

Before Jason can finish his question, Larry interrupts, "It's my house, Toad! Of course I can stop by!"

Jason slowly shakes his head and mumbles to himself, "He is so embarrassing."

Larry reaches into his pant pocket and fumbles around for his car keys. He feverishly unlocks the door and hops into the driver's seat.

"Toad, move it! We have to go!" Larry mutters loudly through the closed window.

Jason desperately struggles to open the enormous car door of the 1983 Lincoln Continental.

After several seconds of a fierce tussle… VICTORY! Jason finally wins the tug-of-war battle against the car door and gets in.

Larry shouts out, "Would you get in the car already? We gotta go! I told you!"

Before Jason can fully close the heavy door, Larry quickly puts the car in reverse and speeds away.

Chapter Two
Move-In Day

I t's a marvelous Saturday afternoon! Bright rays of sunshine shoot down like lasers from the clear blue sky.

Larry's car slowly turns onto Mayfair Court as the newly installed street sign glistens in the sun.

As Larry is driving, there's a conversation occurring inside the car. Like a door-to-door salesman, he is selling the new neighborhood located in Clearwater, Florida to his wife, Ellen.

"I'm telling you, Ellen, this area has THE BEST schools in the country! Everything is brand new and it's all within driving distance. Wait until you see the parks and the shopping centers. The library is enormous! The movie theater has ten separate theaters. Are you kidding me?! There are *five* Chinese restaurants all within three miles. The best part, you ready for this… There's a Denny's we can walk to! It's unbelievable!"

Larry continues to drive down the street until he arrives at his house. He quickly pulls into the brand-new concrete driveway with his family.

Frantically, Larry jumps out of the car and waits in the street to wave down the moving truck driving behind him.

Jason and his brothers Eric, (nicknamed Berry) age five, and Adam, (nicknamed Bub) age three, cautiously step out of the car with looks of amazement on their faces.

Suddenly, filled with exhilaration, they all dart away and begin to dash around their spacious front yard.

Jason leaps onto the large rock used for landscaping.

He faces the street and projects his voice loudly. "The Super Shapiro Brothers are here!"

Once finished, Jason does a flying ninja kick off the rock.

Eric follows by jumping on the same rock and repeating the same line as Jason, "The Super Shapiro Brothers are here!"

He leaps off and is followed by Adam, who does his best to mimic his two older brothers.

"My jump was WAY better than yours, Eric!" brags Jason.

Frowning, Eric lowers his shoulders, and trudges away.

"Hey, don't be a baby, Eric," Jason teases with laughter.

The oversized moving truck is cautiously turning onto May-fair Court and heading to Jason's beautiful new house.

Larry is impatiently pacing back and forth in the middle of the street. He is waving at the driver to park on the side of the road.

The window rolls down and the truck driver politely asks, "Hey, Mr. Shapiro! Can you please move your car out of the driveway so I can back in?"

Aggravated, Larry throws his arms up in the air and responds, "It's a brand-new Lincoln! I have to leave it in the middle of the street?! Unbelievable!"

Reluctantly, Larry re-parks on the side of the street and quickly springs back out of his car.

Ecstatic, he shouts, "Toad, Berry, Bub! Wait until you see the size of the bathrooms. They're massive! The family room has a fireplace and the backyard is the size of a football field. This house is the BEST!"

Everyone sprints into their magnificent new home except Jason. Instead, he decides to stay behind and sit down on the large rock in the front yard.

In awe, Jason smiles as he admires all the custom-built houses and perfectly manicured yards.

Suddenly, he hears the echoing sound of children playing from behind his house. He pauses and listens intently.

Bubbling with curiosity, Jason bolts down the side of his house toward the backyard. He makes his way to a row of freshly planted shrubs that separates his house from the one behind it.

With caution, he slowly peers through the leaves and notices two young boys sprinting down the street. They're playfully squirting a group of young girls with water guns. Laughter fills the air as the girls creatively try to dodge the water, desperately trying not to get wet.

Just as Jason builds up enough courage to take a step through the shrubs, suddenly he hears a roar so loud it rattles the patio screen door.

"TOOOOAD?! WHHHHHHHERE ARE YOUUUUUUU?!"

"Oh, crap!" Jason grumbles as he sprints back to the front of his house.

"Yeah, Dad?" Jason responds as he wipes the sweat off his forehead.

"Come on in! I want you to see your new room! It's humongous!" Larry yells out with joy.

Annoyed, Jason replies, "OK, I'll be right there!"

"You have five minutes, Toad, and then I want you in the house! GOT IT?!" Larry sternly questions.

Frustrated, Jason shouts back, "YEAH! I got it."

Just as Jason begins to head back to the shrubs, out of the corner of his eye, he spots four legs standing on the opposite side of the moving truck. Pausing, Jason bends down and attempts to look underneath the truck.

The first set of legs he sees are small and skinny, wearing scuffed up pink flip flops with a small flower on the top. The second pair of legs appears to be a little bit longer, with golf ball sized knees and wearing the coolest pair of ROOS sneakers Jason had ever seen.

Curious, Jason hesitantly makes his way toward the moving truck. He briskly walks around the cab, in hopes of solving the case of the "mystery legs". As Jason turns the corner, he doesn't see anyone.

"That's so weird," Jason whispers to himself.

Slowly bending down, he peers all the way under the moving truck. Jason sees the same set of four legs, now on the other side of the truck. This time he quickly sprints back around, but no one is there.

"What the heck?" Jason shouts out with confusion. Perplexed, he gives up and decides to walk up his driveway.

Just as he begins to leave, Jason hears giggling and laughing. Quickly, Jason turns around and sees a young boy with the same mushroom-shaped haircut. He is wearing grey shorts and a white tank top, both covered with dirt and grass stains. The little girl has short brown curly hair, wearing denim shorts with a Care Bears T-shirt.

"Hey, what's your name?" questions the boy with curiosity.

"Yeah, what's your name?" repeats the little girl as they both start to chuckle.

Jason hesitantly steps forward and replies, "My name is Jason, but people call me Jay. What's yours?"

"James!" the boy responds, "But you can call me Jimmy."

Jason points to the little girl and asks, "What's your name?"

12

She gazes at Jason, giggles with her hand covering her mouth, and begins to skip down the street.

"Her name is Christina, but you can call her Tina. She's my little annoying sister," Jimmy quickly answers.

"Well, I have a little annoying brother, so we have something in common already. Why did she run away?" Jason questions as he starts to chuckle.

"She gets really embarrassed around boys," Jimmy responds with a grin.

"Hey, are you allowed to come over to my house?" Jimmy questions with eagerness.

"I'm not sure. I'll have to ask my dad. We just moved in today. I haven't even been inside my house yet," Jason replies as the boys laugh in unison.

"Stay here! Let me go check," Jason directs.

Jimmy responds with anticipation, "OK, but hurry up! I wanna show you something!"

Dashing into his house, Jason almost knocks over a moving man walking out of the front door. Upon entering, he instantly feels an overwhelming sense of comfort. Jason can smell the scent of brand-new carpet and freshly painted walls. He notices Eric sorting his baseball cards on the wide-open floor in the family room.

"Where's Daddy?" Jason asks in an agitated tone.

"He's out in the backyard," innocently replies Eric.

With impatience, Jason runs through the house and bursts out of the opened sliding glass door. He sees Larry in the distance at the next-door neighbor's house. He is reclined, relaxing in a lounge chair. Jason decides to cautiously walk over.

There he goes! (Larry is in an animated conversation). We haven't even been here for an hour and he's already made his way into our neighbor's house. My dad would always tread a fine line between being outgoing and the "over-bearing friendly guy" with no social boundaries.

Larry springs off the lounge chair and grabs a cup that was sitting on the patio table. He walks into the neighbor's house, opens the refrigerator, and takes out a gallon of water. He begins to comfortably fill up his cup as the neighbors look at each other shocked and confused.

Casually, Larry walks back out onto the patio and yells to Jason, "Toad! What's going on?! Come inside and say hi to Bruce and Maddie Stevens."

Bruce quickly corrects Larry and reminds him, "It's Pattie!"

Apologetic, Larry swiftly corrects himself, "Oh, sorry Bruce, I mean Pattie!

Jason slowly lifts his hand and gives a slow reserved wave.

"Hey, Dad, a kid down the street just asked if I could play. Can I go over to his house?" asks Jason with anticipation.

"Wow! You're already meeting new friends, Toad! THAT'S SUPER! I told your mom how great this neighborhood is! Yeah, that's fine, go ahead. Just be back in an hour. We're going to Denny's for an early dinner! There's a special on the Grand Slam!" Larry explains with excitement.

"Thanks, Dad!" Jason replies as he quickly waves goodbye to the Stevens. He sprints out of the patio and runs toward his front yard. Breathing heavily, Jason stops and looks around the street but doesn't see Jimmy.

Several kids are riding bikes in the cul-de-sac at the end of the street. Apprehensive, Jason decides to bravely walk toward the group of unknown bike riders.

As Jason approaches, one of the riders quickly darts over, pedaling at full speed. At the last second, the boy on the bike firmly squeezes the handbrake and skids over directly in front of Jason.

There's a baseball card in the back tire between the bicycle spokes.

"Who are you?" the boy questions with concern.

"Um, who are you?" Jason responds in an annoyed tone.

"My name is Kevin. My house is at the top of the street. I know *every* person that lives here."

With sarcasm, Jason replies, "That's really amazing, Kevin! I'm Jason. I just moved in today and I only know *one* person on the street."

"OOF, not good," replies Kevin as he intently stares at Jason with a goofy smile.

Jason asks, "Hey, do you know a kid named Jimmy?"

"Yeah, of course I know him. I told you, I know everyone. He lives over there, in that white house," Kevin responds pointing with the same goofy smile.

"Great, thanks!" responds Jason as he shakes his head and begins to quickly walk toward Jimmy's house.

Kevin yells back, "If you want to be in my bicycle gang, just let me know! Right now, I'm the only member, but I'm recruiting!"

"That sounds awesome! I'll let you know," Jason replies. He then immediately mumbles, "NOT!" to himself as he scampers away.

Relieved, Jason *finally* approaches Jimmy's house.

"Hey! I'm over here!" a voice shouts out.

Confused, Jason cautiously looks around but doesn't see anyone.

"Jay! Over here!"

Jason begins to follow the voice that's heard from the side yard.

"Um, Jimmy, is that you?" Jason yells back as he continues walking.

Unexpectedly, Jason stumbles upon the most breathtaking oak tree he had ever laid eyes on. It is full of the greenest leaves. Sunlight is flickering through the thick branches leaving gorgeous silhouette shadows on the ground.

"I'm up here!" the voice blurts out.

Jason looks up but still doesn't see anyone.

Without any warning, branches begin to feverishly shake and rattle at the top of the tree. Suddenly, Jimmy's head pokes out of the large cluster of leaves.

"So, whatcha think?" Jimmy questions with pride.

"Whoa! How the heck did you get up there?" asks Jason with excitement.

"Come around the other side and I'll show ya!" Jimmy directs.

With immense curiosity, Jason replies, "OK! I'm coming!"

He quickly darts around the tree and then suddenly stops in his tracks with amazement.

"WOW! That's so freaking incredible!" Jason blurts out in awe.

He sees several 2x4's nailed into the tree trunk creating a ladder to climb.

"Come on up!" hollers Jimmy.

"OK, I'm heading up now," Jason responds with a huge grin.

He begins to dart up the 2x4's like a skilled tree climber and makes his way to a flat wooden platform.

"This is so dang cool!" Jason shouts out with joy as he carefully stands up.

"Thanks, I built it a few months ago," Jimmy responds.

"How'd you do it?" questions Jason with curiosity.

Well, I took some of the wood and nails from the house being built across the street. Then, I used my dad's power saw when he was at work. He still hasn't noticed I even built this," Jimmy giggles.

"SO COOL!" Jason replies with a smile.

"Yup! It's pretty awesome if I do say so myself," Jimmy grins with pride.

Suddenly, like a squirrel, Jimmy shoots up the next set of 2x4's to an even higher level in the tree. When he gets to the top, he sits on a smaller hidden platform.

Jimmy shouts back down, "This spot up here, only I can go! It's pretty high up and REALLY dangerous!"

"I can barely see you!" yells Jason.

"Hang on! I'll be back down in a minute!" Jimmy informs.

The top of the tree begins to sway as leaves start to trickle to the ground. Without any warning, Jimmy leaps down onto the lower level platform where Jason is.

"That was sooo cool! You looked like a GI JOE soldier jumping down from a building!" Jason blurts out and both boys start laughing loudly together.

"Jimmy! Honey!" a soothing motherly voice echoes out from the screened-in patio below.

"Yeah, Ma?" loudly responds Jimmy.

"Who's up there with you? I see another person!" asks Jimmy's mother.

"His name is Jason! He just moved in today! He lives on our street!"

"Jimmy, sweetie, come down! Do you want a snack before we leave?" questions his mom.

"YEAH! Coming down now!" Jimmy responds.

"Jay, let's go. My mom's cookies are THE BEST!" he boasts.

The boys scurry back down the tree, open the screen door, and run over to the white PVC patio furniture. They each hop onto a chair and sit down. The outdoor ceiling fan is spinning on high and the kitchen window is wide-open.

"Do you boys want lemonade, or Kool-Aid?" Jimmy's mother questions from the kitchen.

"What do you want, Jay?" Jimmy politely asks.

"I'll have Kool-Aid, but what flavor is it?" questions Jason.

"It's Berry Cherry!" loudly replies Jimmy with confidence.

With a smile, Jason responds, "AWESOME! I LOVE Berry Cherry!"

Moments later, Jimmy's mother cautiously opens the sliding glass door. With a warm sweet smile, she greets Jason and Jimmy with a plastic pitcher of Kool-Aid and a plate of fresh baked cookies. They're still warm from the oven.

"Hi, sweetie, how are you?" questions Jimmy's mother. "My name is Diane Gallo."

"Nice to meet you, Mrs. Gallo," Jason replies.

She clarifies, "So, you just moved in today?"

"Well, the movers are at my house right now. So, we really haven't even moved in yet," Jason mumbles as he eats the homemade cookies with pure contentment.

"That's so exciting! Which house did you move into?" Mrs. Gallo asks with curiosity.

Jason struggles to respond mid-chew, "Its a few houses up the street. It's blue, with a brick front porch."

"Oh, you moved next door to the Stevens. They're very sweet people," she confirms with a smile.

"Yeah, my dad is good friends with them." (Mrs. Gallo has a look of confusion on her face).

"Well, you're going to love living here, honey. It's a fabulous neighborhood and there are lots of kids that live on this street. Jimmy will introduce you to everyone. So, I would love to meet your parents sometime. Do you have any brothers or sisters?" Mrs. Gallo inquires in a caring tone.

"I have two brothers. Their names are Berry and Bub," Jason grins as he responds.

"Berry and Bub?" Mrs. Gallo questions for clarification while chuckling.

"Yeah, my dad has nicknames for all of us. My nickname is Toad."

Mrs. Gallo laughs and replies, "He must be some character if he came up with all of those names for you boys."

"Yup! He is, but sometimes he can be sooo embarrassing! Overall, he's a good dad, I guess," Jason responds with a shoulder shrug.

"Awww... That's very sweet. Well, Jimmy has to go visit his grandfather, so we're going to be leaving soon. You're welcome back here anytime, sweetheart. Jimmy, say goodbye to Jason and go write down your phone number for him," directs Mrs. Gallo as she walks back inside the house.

"OK, Ma!" shouts Jimmy has he sprints into the kitchen to grab a pen and paper. He quickly returns and hands Jason a ripped corner of a magazine. "Here's my number, Jay. I'm going to pull out my bike ramp tomorrow if you want to come over. Do you have a bike?" Jimmy questions.

"Yeah! I have a MONGOOSE," Jason states with pride.

"Cool, what color?" Jimmy inquires.

"It's blue with matching tires and silver pegs on the back. My little butthead brother Eric has a red one. It's the color I actually wanted," Jason informs with frustration.

"Jeez, Jay, it sounds like you don't like your brother too much. Well, my bike is a DIAMONDBACK. It's black, with pegs on the front AND BACK!" Jimmy boasts.

"SON! Say goodbye, NOW! We're leaving!" yells out Jimmy's dad with the tone of an angry marine drill sergeant.

"I gotta go. I'll see you later. I don't want my dad to ground me for a week. You can leave through the screen door," Jimmy directs.

"OK. I'll see you later!" Jason shouts as he walks out of the patio door waving goodbye.

"Hey, Jay… I'm glad you moved here," Jimmy responds with a warm smile.

Jason replies with certainty, "Me too," as he starts to head home.

On the way he pauses and intently stares at the tree house with admiration.

Jason makes his way onto the sidewalk at the same time Mr. Gallo is pulling out of the driveway in his 1982 Blue Buick Regal. Jimmy and his sister turn around and wave through the back window as they drive away. Tina playfully sticks her tongue out as Jason laughs and shakes his head.

> And that was the day I met my best friend. It's amazing how lifelong friendships can start from the most unexpected places, at the most random times. You see, back in the summer of 1983 every day was an adventure. There weren't cell phones or home computers yet. There wasn't Facebook. The Internet... What the hell was that? (laughing) Most importantly, I'm happy to report there were definitely, NO playdates! You simply walked outside and played with whoever happened to be there. You got into arguments and then always seemed to eventually work it out. When you got hurt, your friends would all pitch in and carry you home. Your mother would simply point to the ice packs when you walked through the door. Then when you woke up the next morning, you got to do it all over again. Were the 80's the last great decade to be a kid? If you'd ask me, I would tell you it was.

Early evening sets in as Jason walks back to his house. He eagerly opens the front door and strolls past several moving boxes neatly stacked against the side of the wall.

"I'm home!" Jason proudly shouts.

"Toad, you've been gone for hours! Where were you?" Larry wonders with excitement.

Elated, Jason responds, "I met a kid that lives at the end of the street! His name is Jimmy!"

"That's OUTSTANDING, Toad! See, we haven't even been here for a day and you've already made a new friend. Listen,

Mommy unpacked your clothes and put them on your bed. No showers tonight. Go outside and rinse off in the pool. We're going to go to Denny's for an early dinner! I have a coupon for a *free* Grand Slam! You and your brothers can split it," Larry explains with enthusiasm.

Jason shakes his head and mutters, "Rinse off in the pool?" Begrudgingly, he grabs a towel out of a moving box, opens the sliding glass door and then flings it closed. Jason walks towards the pool. The sun's golden rays are reflecting on the calm water surface. Looking up, Jason stares deep into the piercing blue sky. He then takes a deep breath, holds his nose, and smiles with contentment. Suddenly, Jason does a massive cannonball into the deep-end of the pool.

Chapter Three
Candy Bar Frisbees

Night falls, as the Shapiros arrive home from Denny's. Larry's newly polished Lincoln pulls into the driveway. All the doors simultaneously open and everyone feverishly exits the car.

Larry shouts out, "Ellen, don't forget the bags with the food in it!"

"I can't believe you actually asked to take home the food you sent back, Larry. It's so embarrassing!" Ellen scolds as she takes three Denny's plastic bags out of the car.

"They were going to throw it away!" responds Larry with a chuckle.

Everyone dashes through the front door and flops onto the couch in the family room. Larry turns on the television and the movie CHARIOTS OF FIRE is playing on HBO.

"Go get ready for bed, guys!" Larry directs.

The three boys run into their rooms. After several minutes, they sprint back out into a single file line all wearing superhero UNDEROOS. Larry gets up and dashes over to the refrigerator. He grabs three candy bars from the pullout drawer and proceeds to toss them like frisbees from the kitchen, all the way into the family room.

"There's your dessert, guys!" Larry shouts with laughter.

"Jesus, Larry! They're not farm animals!" Ellen scolds with annoyance.

Jason and Eric instantly start bickering over who will get the mouthwatering Mounds bar.

"Give it to me, Eric, NOW!" demands Jason.

"NO! STOP! I had it first! It's mine!" Eric cries out.

Jason knocks him down and shouts out, "You're so annoying! I can't stand you!"

Starting to sob, Eric wipes the tears from his eyes.

Larry runs over and screams, "Knock it off or you're going to be punished, Jason!"

"It wasn't me! It was him!" Jason replies as he adamantly points to five-year-old, Eric.

"I don't care! You're the oldest and you should know better!" Larry explains with frustration.

"Ugh! I just can't stand him!" yells Jason as he stamps his foot.

Larry abruptly escorts Jason to the corner of the room and demands, "LISTEN TO ME! I have told you before and I will tell you again! Your brothers are the most important people in your life! One day you'll realize that!"

"I really don't care!" yells Jason as he runs into his bedroom, slamming the door closed.

Eric is left sitting on the couch by himself, devouring his candy bar of choice with pure happiness. Chocolate is covering his freckled face as he looks up and smiles with complete satisfaction.

Chapter Four

Jimmy Visits

The Next Morning

Unexpectedly, the doorbell rings, followed by several soft knocks. Larry stumbles out of his bedroom visibly irritated as he stomps toward the front door. The digital clock on the oven displays that it is 7:00 AM.

Accidentally, Larry stubs his toe on a moving box that is stacked along the wall. He lets out a yelp while struggling to stay quiet. Quickly opening the front door, Larry walks outside onto the porch.

"Can I help you?" Larry asks with frustration.

A young, dark-haired boy is innocently standing next to his bike.

"Is Jay home?" the boy casually asks as he looks up.

"Do you know how early it is?" quizzes Larry as he yawns.

"Why are you still in your undies?" the boy genuinely asks with a chuckle.

Larry looks down and replies with a serious tone, "Because it's my house!"

"Can Jay play?" questions the boy as he grins at Jason's father.

With curiosity, Larry asks, "What's your name?"

"My name is Jimmy. I live down the street."

"Well, nice to meet you, Jimmy. I'm Larry Shapiro. You can come in, but next time, wait until it's 9:00 o'clock before you start banging on my door. Got it?" questions Larry with frustration.

"OK! Thanks Larry," replies Jimmy.

"You mean thanks, Mr. Shapiro?" Larry responds with a playful scowl.

Jimmy enters the house and walks over to the hallway where the bedrooms are located. He quietly opens each door and peers inside until he finds Jason's room. Cautiously walking in, Jimmy stands next to the bed. He softly requests Jason to wake up.

"Jay," Jimmy whispers.

A blurry image of Jimmy is seen through Jason's eyes.

"Jimmy?" Jason responds in a groggy morning voice.

"Yeah, it's me," Jimmy confirms.

"What time is it?" Jason replies as he begins to stretch like a cat waking up from a nap.

Looking at his PAC-MAN digital watch, Jimmy replies, "Its 7:10 in the morning."

Now fully awake, Jason questions with excitement, "Who the heck let you inside this early?"

"Your dad did!" Jimmy confirms.

"Let me guess… He answered the door in his underwear?" asks Jason with embarrassment.

"Yup! He sure did!" Jimmy responds out loud with laughter. Both boys giggle.

"He upsets me all the time. He's ALWAYS doing stupid things like that!" Jason adamantly confirms as he sits up.

"Go get dressed and meet me outside. I pulled out my ramp! We can jump our bikes off of it!" Jimmy blurts out with excitement.

"AWESOME! I can't wait to try it!" Jason shouts as he leaps out of his bed with joy.

Jimmy turns and walks out of Jason's room. As he wanders through the family room, he sees Eric relaxing on a wicker Papasan chair watching TV. He's eating Smurf Berry Crunch out of the cereal box with two hands at the same time. As he grabs each handful, piles of cereal fill the chair's cushion.

Jimmy waves and smiles.

Eric opens both fists which are full of cereal and waves back. The carpet quickly becomes covered with the crunchy berry pebbles.

Jimmy calls over to Eric, "Hey! You're a hungry little fella!"

With a big smile, Eric replies, "I'm always hungry!" showing all his missing teeth.

Jimmy laughs as he comfortably strolls out of the front door. Shortly after, Jason jogs through the family room. He stops, looks at Eric, and reprimands him with an angry tone, "LOOK WHAT YOU DID! You got cereal all over the place. You're going to be punished when mommy sees this, Eric. You're the worst!"

Eric pauses from eating, looks at Jason with a defeated face and yells back, "You're so mean!"

Larry hears the arguing from his bedroom. He charges out through the door, still wearing only his underwear.

"What the hell is going on, Jason?" Larry roars.

Both boys begin aggressively talking over each other.

Loudly, Larry demands, "BE QUIET! Adam and your mom are sleeping. Eric, go to your room. Jason, get out of here now

27

and go to Jimmy's. We will discuss this disgusting behavior later! You're going to be punished for a week. I swear!"

Jason stomps out of the house, pauses, and yells back with anger, "ERIC, I CAN'T STAND YOU!"

Jason's little brother has tears streaming down his face as he gets up and walks to his room.

With concern, Larry questions, "Why are you crying, Berry?"

Eric pauses, looks at his father and says, "Daddy, he hates me."

"Berry, come here," Larry requests with a sensitive tone. He kneels down and affectionately puts his arm around Eric's shoulder.

"Jason doesn't hate you. Sometimes older brothers get used to being the only child and receiving all the attention. Once you and Adam were born, we had to take care of all of you. Sometimes I think Jason gets angry about that. I'll talk to him. Don't be upset, pal. We're going to go to the movies today! If you're good, I'll let you pick out one candy bar from the store and sneak it in the theater."

Still visibly upset, Eric responds, "OK, Daddy."

"Come on Berry, a nice candy bar will make you feel better, right?"

Eric looks up at Larry with a big smile and responds, "Can I get *two* candy bars?"

"Awww… Now that's what I like to hear. Listen, I'll talk to Jason about being more patient with you," Larry promises.

In a soft tone, Eric replies, "Thanks, Daddy."

My father always had this theory. Since I was the oldest and was the "first born", I always had animosity toward my brother Eric for taking the attention away from me. Now, whether that's true or not, I have to admit, I wasn't very nice to him. In fact, there were times I was downright mean. You see, when you're eight years old, you don't realize how you treat people today can impact someone's life tomorrow. You don't realize that words can lift someone up or bring someone crashing down. You don't realize kindness is the most important quality someone can possess. And you *definitely* don't realize that guilt can creep up very quietly many years later when you least expect it.

The Magic of Mayfair

Chapter Five

Meeting Donnie

Jason walks toward Jimmy's house and suddenly sees an awesome aerodynamic bike ramp in the distance.

"WOW! Sooo cool!" Jason says to himself in amazement.

All of a sudden, out of the corner of Jason's eye, he sees a blur blaze by him. He hears the words, "WATCH THIS!" It's Jimmy zooming by on his shiny new DIAMONDBACK bicycle. He hits the ramp full speed, soars through the air, and lands perfectly as he glides around the cul-de-sac with absolute ease.

"That was awesome! You're amazing!" Jason yells out as he sprints toward Jimmy.

"Thanks! It really isn't a big deal. If you think that was cool, check this out!" Jimmy brags as he aggressively pedals back up the street.

"What are you going to do now?" Jason yells out with anticipation.

"Just watch!" Jimmy shouts back and winks.

Jason responds, "OK!" as he jumps up and down with exhilaration.

"Here he comes!" yells out a deep, preadolescent voice from behind Jason.

Mesmerized, Jason can't take his eyes off of Jimmy.

As fast as a jet airplane, Jimmy pedals down the street at mock speed. Jason begins cheering with joy and admiration.

Just as Jimmy approaches, he pulls his front wheel up and proceeds to execute the longest wheelie Jason had ever seen. It seems like an eternity that Jimmy is coasting on his back tire before landing gracefully on the ground.

"Oh, man, that was so awesome!" Jason exclaims.

"Nice job, Jimmy!" the unknown voice blurts out again.

"Thanks, guys! Hey, Jay, this is my friend Donnie. He lives on the street behind us. He always cuts through my backyard," Jimmy informs while high-fiving the tall, stout boy standing behind Jason.

With curiosity Jason replies, "Wow, really?"

"Yeah, Donnie should be in fifth grade, but he got held back by his *mommy*. He's in fourth grade with me," Jimmy teases with laughter.

Embarrassed, Donnie responds, "Real funny, Jim."

"Dude, relax! I'm just kidding! It's not my fault that you look like André the Giant," Jimmy jokes as he chuckles.

Donnie shakes his head and desperately tries to change the subject.

"So… Did you just move here, Jay?" Donnie quickly questions as he wipes the sweat off his forehead with the bottom of his t-shirt.

"Yeah, I just moved into my house yesterday," responds Jason with enthusiasm.

"That's really cool!" replies Donnie with excitement.

"JIMMY!!!!!"

"Oh, crap, that's my dad," Jimmy nervously confirms.

32

"What the hell are you doing jumping your bike off that ramp this early in the morning? Put it back in the garage right now before I throw it into the fireplace!" Mr. Gallo fiercely yells out.

"OK, Dad, relax, calm down!" Jimmy attempts to reason.

"NOW!" screams out Mr. Gallo with an intense roar.

"OK, OK! Guys, do me a favor and help me lift this ramp up. We need to move it back into my garage before my dad goes crazy!" Jimmy nervously requests.

"Got it!" Jason and Donnie reply in unison.

Just as the boys lift up the ramp, a voice that sounds like it was projected from a megaphone is heard.

"JAAASSSSOOON!!!"

"OH MY GOD! He is so damn embarrassing!" Jason mumbles as he clenches his teeth together.

"TOAD! LET'S GO!" Larry yells out as he begins to walk down the street.

The boys scurry into the garage with the ramp and drop it on the ground.

"Listen... I gotta go. My dad is out of control!" Jason blurts out with frustration.

"Wow! Your dad is so loud!" Donnie replies giggling.

"Yeah, I know. He always does this. I'll see you guys later," replies Jason as he begins to trudge down the driveway.

"Knock on my door if you can play later. I should be home," informs Jimmy.

"Hey, Jay, who's Toad by the way?" asks Donnie as he hysterically laughs.

"Unfortunately, it's my nickname. My dad has nicknames for everyone. Yours might be smelly since you're sweating like a pig," jokes Jason as he chuckles.

Red-faced, Donnie shakes his head and proceeds to light up a cigarette in front of Jimmy's house.

> That was Donnie. His parents had recently gotten divorced and he was basically raising himself. You see, back in the early 1980's, children from separated families were looked at as "troubled" or "the kid you didn't want your kid" hanging out with. Donnie was a good person, but when your mother gives you a key to the house and tells you she's going to her boyfriends for the weekend, it's a lot of freedom for a ten-year-old to handle.

Jason charges toward his father, who is now halfway down the street, continuing to shout.

"TOAD! Come here! I have fantastic news!" Larry shares with excitement.

"What, Dad? I was actually having fun! Why are you calling me? Also, stop yelling out Toad so everyone can hear it. It's embarrassing! I'm eight years old. I'm not a little kid anymore," Jason replies with frustration.

"Sorry, Toad. While you live in my house, I can call you anything I want," Larry declares with a chuckle.

"So what's this 'great news' about, Dad?" questions Jason sarcastically.

"Mommy just got off the phone with Nanny Gloria. Your grandparents are coming up to visit this week! They'll be here Thursday and they'll stay through Sunday. They want to see the new house and I guess you guys too," Larry laughs as he playfully flicks Jason's earlobe.

"Not cool, Dad!" Jason angrily responds.

"Hey, I'm going to take Eric to the movies in a little bit to see THE RETURN OF THE JEDI. Do you want to go, too?" Larry invites.

"Only if I can get SNO-CAPS, popcorn, and a cherry COKE." Jason fiercely negotiates.

"I'm not buying candy at the movies, Toad! Are you kidding me? It's a total rip off! You can run inside ECKERD and pick out a few snacks. I can buy *four* candy bars for the price of one at the theater," Larry explains with enthusiasm.

"Fine, I'll go," Jason begrudgingly confirms.

"Don't do me any favors, Toad. You better be nice to your brother." Larry gently pokes Jason on his shoulder. "He looks up to you. You're his older brother. You never know what can happen in life. Imagine how bad you would feel if something ever happened to that cute little guy. Jason… Look at me, I'm serious, man. I mean it. In this world, the only people you can count on are your brothers. Don't you ever forget that," Larry instructs with heartfelt compassion.

"Fine," Jason responds haphazardly.

"No, it's not *fine*. It's very important! DAMN IT!" Larry yells out with frustration.

There's an emotional pause as Larry struggles to catch his breath.

"We need to get going to the movie. It starts in less than three hours. We also have to stop and pick up the candy on the way. I'll be in the car waiting. Go get your brother, NOW!" Larry demands with intensity.

Jason jogs up the driveway, opens the front door, and yells out with a loud obnoxious voice, "Eric! Let's go! We're leaving, now! Daddy's waiting for you!"

Quickly darting back to the car, Jason waits in the passenger seat to leave. Eric walks out shortly after and struggles to open the heavy car door.

"Really nice, Jason, you couldn't get out and help your brother open the stinkin' car door? See, this is *exactly* what I'm talking about!" Larry shouts out with frustration.

Annoyed, Larry leaps out of the car and lets Eric inside. He gets back in, pulls out of the driveway, and speeds up the street.

Chapter Six

Jason's Grandparents Visit

A gorgeous metallic blue Cadillac turns onto Mayfair Court, slowly stopping in front of every other house looking for Jason's address.

The three boys are all lined up in a row, kneeling on the couch in the living room. They're peering through the window blinds, anxiously waiting for the "arrival honk" of their grandparents.

With excitement, Jason yelps out, "I can't wait to see what Nanny got us! Hopefully I get a new HE-MAN figure."

Eric responds in a squeaky five year old's voice, "I hope it's arts and crafts supplies!"

Adam blurts out, "Well, I hope she got me a puppy dog!"

"You're funny, Adam. Nanny and Poppy wouldn't get you a dog," Jason corrects with a smile.

"Well, maybe. You never know," replies Eric.

"You're so dumb, Eric! I'm not even talking to you anymore," Jason yells out.

"Hey, hey, hey! Knock it off, Jason. You won't be getting ANY presents if you don't behave! Get over here!" yells Larry.

Dragging his feet with both arms crossed, Jason slowly walks toward his dad.

Annoyed and frustrated, he questions, "What?"

"I'm not going to tell you again about being kind to your brother," Larry demands.

"Well, he started it!" Jason tattles.

With an upset tone, Larry states, "Well, I'm tired of it! If it doesn't stop right now, you're going to be punished for the entire week. No TV and no ATARI! Got it?"

Angrily, Jason replies, "Yeah, fine!"

Setting expectations, Larry demands, "I don't want any trouble while your grandparents are here. DO YOU UNDERSTAND ME?!"

"Yeah… Fine, Dad," Jason agrees with annoyance.

Without any warning, the doorbell rings! The boys flock to the front door like pigeons at a park.

"I want to get the door. No, I want to get it!" All the boys bicker over who is going to open the door first.

Jason shoves Eric to the side as he begins to sob. Eric trudges over to the couch and sits down by himself.

"Hello Nanny, Hello Poppy. Please, come on in," Jason welcomes his grandparents like a young salesman while opening the front door.

"Hi Nanny! Hi Poppy!" repeats three-year-old Adam.

"Awww… Hi boys. Come give us a hug," requests Nanny Gloria.

"Where's Eric?" immediately questions Poppy Al.

Whimpering, Eric replies, "I'm over here, on the couch."

"What's the matter, sweetie?" questions Nanny with concern.

Frowning, Eric responds, "Well, Jason pushed me."

"That certainly wasn't nice! Get over here and give Nanny a hug. Come with us to put our luggage down. We got you boys a few little presents," Nanny Gloria explains.

"OK, Nanny," responds Eric with a grin.

Without warning, Larry flies around the corner wearing only underwear and a polo shirt. He passionately bear hugs Al and Gloria.

"Ellen! Your parents are here!" Larry shouts out with excitement.

Everyone piles into the family room and lounges on the grey corduroy couch.

"Guys, give your grandparents a chance to relax before you start begging for toys. Unreal!" shouts Larry as he throws up his arms in the air.

Poppy Al announces, "OK, before we give you anything, I want to know all about your new house and this beautiful neighborhood. Eric, what do you like most?"

"Um, I like the backyard, Poppy. I can throw my baseball with my dad."

With frustration, Jason corrects, "You mean throw MY autographed Mike Schmidt ball that you, RUINED!"

"Oh boy, that's not good. Adam, what about you?" questions Poppy Al.

With intense thought, Adam replies, "Let's see... I like my pool. I went swimming this morning and sat on my alligator float."

Nanny Gloria smiles and replies, "That's great, honey! I can't wait to see you swim!"

"Jason, what about you? What do you like most about living here?" Nanny joyfully questions.

"Well, I already met my best friend!" Jason answers with conviction.

"Wow! Really? That's fabulous!" responds Nanny Gloria.

"Yup! His name is Jimmy. He lives at the end of our street. We're basically like brothers," declares Jason.

"You just met him, Toad! He can't be your best friend that quickly," Larry reminds.

"I know, Dad, but trust me, we're best friends!" Jason adamantly confirms.

"OK, OK, fine. You're best friends," responds Larry as he shakes his head.

"Hi Mom, hi Dad," a soft-spoken voice echoes from the next room. Ellen walks into the family room and gently hugs both of her parents.

"Hello, Ellen. You look fantastic! I guess these boys are keeping you active. How are you doing, sweetheart?" Nanny Gloria inquires.

"Oh, I'm good. Yes, they're keeping me very busy. I don't even have time to think most days," Ellen replies as she chuckles.

"Excuse me, Nanny, but Adam wants to know if we can have our toys," Jason interrupts with eagerness.

"Hmm… I think it's actually Mr. Jason who wants to know if he can have his toys," chuckles Nanny Gloria.

"Al, do me a favor and look in the blue suitcase. Can you grab me the KAY-BEE TOYS bag?" instructs Nanny Gloria.

Poppy Al shuffles through the piece of luggage and grabs an enormous plastic bag that is overflowing with goodies. He hands it to Nanny Gloria. Immediately after, he begins to carefully unzip a brown leather carrying case. With great pride, Poppy Al reveals his brand-new 1983 Rolleiflex thirty-five-millimeter camera. He starts intensely snapping photos of all his grandchildren.

"Wow! That's a really awesome camera, Poppy," Jason compliments with amazement.

All the boys quickly line up like soldiers standing at attention in anticipation of receiving their presents.

40

"OK, I'm going to start with the youngest," Nanny Gloria announces with a warm smile.

Under his breath, Jason mumbles, "Darn it!"

"OK, Adam… Let's see what Nanny and Poppy have for you," exclaims Jason's grandmother.

She unveils a blue punch balloon, a Smurfs coloring book, and a Scooby Doo puzzle.

"What do you say, Adam?" questions Ellen.

Like a dog panting, Adam replies, "Thank you!"

"OK, who's next?" questions Nanny as she scans the room.

Leaping up and down, Jason yells out, "ME! ME! ME!" as he stretches his arm as high as it can go.

"Eric, come here, honey," requests Nanny Gloria.

Jason grits his teeth and grumbles, "DANG IT!"

With excitement, Nanny Gloria pulls out a G.I. JOE action figure, scented magic markers, and an Inspector Gadget coloring book.

"This is so awesome, Nanny! Thank you!" Eric shouts out with joy.

"OK, last but certainly not least… Come on down, Mr. Jason!" Nanny Gloria announces like a game show host.

Jason bows and questions with excitement, "What did you get me?"

Nanny reaches deep into the white plastic bag and pulls out a math workbook and colored pencils.

With a confused look, Jason quickly makes eye contact with his father and then questions, "Really, Nanny, no toy?"

Laughing, Nanny Gloria responds, "OK, I think there might be one more toy for you, Jason."

She proudly reaches back into the bag, takes out a brand-new HE-MAN action figure, and hands it to Jason.

"YES! MOSS MAN! AWESOME!!! I wanted him so bad!" Jason confirms with elation as he bounces up and down.

With enthusiasm, Nanny announces, "And… I have one more present that is for all of you!"

"Is it a camera, like Poppy has? I want one so badly!" blurts out Jason with excitement.

"I'm sorry, sweetheart, it's not a camera," responds Nanny Gloria with sincere disappointment.

She reaches deep into her bag and pulls out a shiny white baseball with bright red stitching.

"This is for all of you to share and have fun with," Nanny specifically instructs.

Jason dashes over and immediately snatches the baseball from his grandmother's hand.

"Hey! That ball is for all of you, Jason. Do you even know where your baseball mitt is?" questions Larry.

"Yeah, it's in my closet," replies Jason with certainty.

"Al, I think there's one more piece of luggage in the car. Can you please go grab it?" politely requests Nanny Gloria.

"Yup, I'll go get it. Larry come with me, I'll show you the new Cadillac! We just got it last week," Al invites with a smile.

"CADDY?! Ah, you didn't end up getting the Lincoln? They're such a better deal right now with all the rebates and incentives!" Larry informs with exhilaration.

Al rolls his eyes and shakes his head in disbelief at Larry's response. They both walk outside and casually stroll down the driveway.

"Wow! Great color, Al! The metallic blue you got is really nice, but to be honest, grey holds up much better," Larry attempts to compliment.

"Umm, thanks. It really drove like a dream on the way over here. We actually bought the more expensive model. It has the 4.1 L V-8 engine," Al replies as he admires his beauty with both hands on his hips.

"I'm sure it handles great, but you really gotta drive my Lincoln. It's so quiet! You can't even tell it's running. But it is beautiful, Al, really it is. Mazel Tov! Use it in good health."

With pride, Al opens the car door and responds, "Check out that leather," as he grabs the last piece of luggage.

"Wow! Those seats look really comfortable. When you test drive my car though, you'll see Lincoln goes with *slightly* higher-grade leather. Again, it's a great looking car, Al! Oh, when you can, I would pull her up into the driveway so she's not parked in the street," Larry reminds.

"I'm going to take a quick walk. I'll move her onto the driveway before I head back inside. Can you bring in this suitcase and let Gloria know I'll be back in a little bit? I'm going to go smoke a cigarette. It's been a busy day. These long drives stress me out," Al responds with a deep breath.

"Spend a few days in my house and you'll be smoking the entire pack!" Larry chuckles.

Just as Larry darts into the house, Jason and Eric squeeze through the front door at the same exact time. They have their leather baseball mitts under their arms and quickly "take the field" in their front yard.

"OK, you stand over there, Eric. I'll stand here," Jason strictly instructs.

The boys separate about twenty feet apart. Jason takes the brand-new baseball out of his mitt and begins to toss grounders to his brother.

"Eric! Let's pretend to be Major League baseball players. I'll be Mike Schmidt. Who are you?" Jason questions with curiosity.

"Well, I like the Chicago Cubs. I'll be Ryne Sandberg," Eric decides as he pounds the inside of his mitt.

"OK, Eric, I'm gonna throw you a ground ball and then throw it back to me. Got it? Do you understand?" Jason questions.

With confidence, Eric responds, "Yup, I got it!"

The boys proceed to playfully throw the ball to each other for the next several minutes.

"Hey, Eric, watch how high I can throw the baseball," Jason brags.

He steps back, winds up his arm, and throws the ball as if it was shot out of a circus cannon! The baseball hits the ground about fifty yards behind Eric. It takes a high bounce and then begins to steadily roll down the street.

"Eric, hurry up! Go get the ball before it goes into the sewer!" Jason sternly directs.

"OK! I got it!" replies Eric, as he sprints full speed after the ball.

"Don't let it go into the sewer, Eric! RUN FASTER!" Jason screams out.

The ball continues to roll down the street as it begins to rapidly gain speed.

"RUN FASTER! It's going to fall into the sewer, Eric! You better get it, or you're going to be in BIG trouble!" shouts Jason.

Breathing heavily, Eric tries with all his might to propel his little legs fast enough to grab the ball before it is lost forever.

Just before the ball rolls into the sewer, Eric dives into the air like a baseball player stealing home plate. With his hand stretched out, Eric manages to get one finger on the ball, right before it enters the sewer.

The baseball is safe! Eric gradually gets up. His face is blistering red and covered in sweat. His knees are scraped and bloodied from the asphalt. Eric turns and holds the ball up in victory as he smiles with immense relief.

"I got it! I did it!" Eric proudly announces with excitement.

"Good job! You saved the day!" Jason *finally* compliments.

Eric sprints over and excitedly hands the ball back to his big brother. He pauses, stares Jason in the eyes, and hugs him.

"Are you proud of me?" Eric questions with uncertainty. Not sure how to respond, Jason looks Eric in the eyes.

The anticipation of Jason's first heartfelt emotional response builds as there's a short pause.

"Um… Here, just take the ball, Eric. Go back over to the side of the yard and throw it to me," Jason uncomfortably instructs.

Eric pauses as he looks down at the ground and follows Jason's directions with defeat.

"Hey! Throw me the ball as high as you can!" Jason requests.

"OK, sure," Eric responds sobbing as he gets into his throwing stance. He looks down at the ball and holds it in his hand. Suddenly, with all his built-up emotion, Eric launches the ball with every ounce of strength he has.

The baseball climbs to its peak in the air just as Jason's grandfather is returning back from his walk.

Instantly, there's a strong breeze that changes the ball's trajectory in mid-air. Poppy Al happens to notice the scene unfolding as the baseball gradually begins to drift over the brand-new Caddy. He quickly realizes the ball is on target for a direct *hood hit!*

Pure terror can be seen in Jason and Eric's faces as they attempt to process what is about to happen.

The boy's line of sight shifts between the baseball and Poppy Al as the intense incident continues to unfold.

Once the baseball is perfectly centered over the car, what looks and feels like a twenty-pound bowling ball suddenly drops out of the sky and slams onto the hood!

"GLORIA!!!" Poppy Al yells so loud that his voice can be heard from inside the house.

The neighbors begin to peer through their window blinds to see what all the commotion is about.

"Eric, WHAT DID YOU DO?! You're going to be in big trouble!" screeches Jason so loudly his voice cracks.

"GLORIA!" Poppy Al continues to shriek.

The front door flies opened and Jason's grandmother comes dashing outside.

She franticly questions, "What's the matter, Al? Why are you screaming so loud?"

"They dented the GOD DAMN car, Glor! Look at this!" Poppy Al yells as he points to the dent with pure agony.

Calmly, Nanny Gloria responds, "OK, it's a dent. Relax, we will get it fixed. I thought one of the boys hurt themselves the way you were carrying on."

With a sad, whimpering voice, Eric apologizes, "Poppy, I'm so sorry. I didn't mean to do this. Please forgive me."

Al reassures, "Don't worry, buddy. Give me a hug. I know you didn't mean to put a giant dent right in the middle of the hood."

"Eric, I can't believe you did that!" Jason reprimands as everyone walks back into the house.

"Hey, Jason, that's not very nice! It was an accident. Take it easy on your brother," Nanny Gloria scolds in a firm voice.

"I'm going over to Jimmy's house," Jason responds as he blatantly ignores his grandmother.

"Be back in an hour! We're going to eat dinner at six o'clock sharp! Got it?" Larry shouts.

"Yeah, fine," Jason replies back with a defeated tone.

> For the first time in my life, I felt really bad for my little brother. I actually regretted blaming him for crushing my grandfather's dream of what a "perfect car" looked like. Man, did he work hard to save that baseball from the depths of the smelly, wet sewer. He really just wanted me to be proud of what he did. I'm honestly not sure why I was always so hard on him. My father would always declare that deep down I was upset Eric took the attention away from me when he was born. I don't really know if that was true, but what I do know, is that all he wanted was my attention and validation.
>
> That was also the day guilt made its first appearance and it was resting heavily in my heart. I wasn't quite sure what it was yet, but I knew it was something I was beginning to struggle with.

Jason approaches the Gallo's house and sees Jimmy pushing his lawn mower into the garage.

"Hey! What's going on?" yells out Jason from the bottom of the driveway.

"I just finished cutting the grass!" responds Jimmy with pride.

"Wait, you're actually allowed to cut your own grass?" Jason questions as he stares intently at the lawnmower.

"When I turned nine, my dad made me do it. He starts the mower for me, but I push it. It's not hard," Jimmy says as he proudly flexes his biceps.

"Wow, that's cool! Even though your muscles look like little tiny marshmallows," Jason snickers.

"Does your dad cut your lawn?" questions Jimmy.

Laughing uncontrollably, Jason replies, "NO WAY! My dad can barely change a light bulb!"

"Well, I guess that's a good thing. The neighbors wouldn't want to see him cutting your lawn in his undies and dress shoes," Jimmy chuckles as he pushes the mower to the side of the garage.

With laughter, Jason agrees, "Yeah... That would just be scary!"

"Hey, wanna go hang out in the tree house?" suggests Jimmy. The boys smile at each other and instantly dash out of the garage to the side yard.

Jimmy springs up the 2x4's nailed to the tree and crawls onto the first level platform.

Looking down, Jimmy yells out, "Come on up, Jay. It's awesome up here!"

"OK, I'm coming!" Jason responds as he shoots up each 2X4 like a squirrel, quickly making his way to the platform.

"Look, I brought up my radio! I'll put on some music. I also have some snacks up here for us," Jimmy shouts as he grabs a plastic KASH N' KARRY bag.

"Oh man! What do you have?" questions Jason with curiosity.

Purposely opening the bag slowly, Jimmy proudly recites, "I have MOON PIES, I have DEVIL DOGS, I have SWISS CAKE ROLLS, and I have FRUIT ROLL-UPS."

Jumping up and down with amazement, Jason asks, "Where the heck did you get all of this from? It looks like you bought everything on the snack aisle. I can't believe this!"

"Shhh… Keep it down, Jay. I went into my pantry closet and took a little bit of everything. You want something?" whispers Jimmy.

"Heck, yeah I do!" Jason pauses. "Oh, dang it! I have to eat dinner soon. My dad will kill me if he finds out I had snacks now," Jason whines with frustration.

"Well, I'm starving," Jimmy announces as he tears open the box of MOON PIES like a madman.

After a few minutes of watching Jimmy indulge himself with delicious treats, Jason can no longer resist. He loses control and digs into the SWISS CAKE ROLLS. Jason begins to carefully peal the chocolate off the cream filling.

While chewing a mouth full of cake, Jason mumbles to Jimmy, "This tree house is sooo amazing. I feel like we're away from everyone. The breeze feels so nice up here."

Nodding his head, Jimmy shares, "You know… Sometimes I come up here and just think about stuff. It calms me down when I get nervous or upset. I wonder what things will be like when I'm older. I think about my parents… I think about my sisters… I think about my friends…"

"Really?" questions Jason with surprise.

With appreciation, Jimmy responds, "Yeah… Ya know… I'm really lucky you moved here, Jay. I feel like we've known each other for years even though we just met."

"I know, it's weird. I feel like we've been friends for a really long time. Almost like we're brothers," Jason vividly imagines.

Jimmy laughs and responds, "Yeah, I always wanted a brother."

"Jimmy?" a voice yells out from the patio below.

With caution, Jimmy responds, "WHAT?" as he kneels down and frantically hides all the boxes of snacks.

"Did you go into the pantry again? I told you to stop doing that! Those are all the snacks for the entire month. Why'd you do that, honey? Now there's not going to be anything left!" Mrs. Gallo questions with frustration.

"JIMMY!?!?" another voice shouts out even louder with an agitated tone.

"Get your ass in here NOW, before I go out there and grab you! You have one minute!" instructs Mr. Gallo as the sliding glass door slams shut.

"Dang, he's pissed! Every time I empty the pantry I get in big trouble," advises Jimmy.

"Well, why do you keep doing it?" questions Jason with confusion.

"I don't know. I like snacks," Jimmy replies, shrugging his shoulders as he giggles.

"JAAASSSSOOON! JAAASSSSOOON!!"

"What the heck is that yelling your name?!" Jimmy asks with concern.

"It's just my dad," Jason responds as he shakes his head and takes a deep breath.

"JAAASSSOOON! DINNNER TIME!!"

Jimmy covers his ears and responds, "WOW! He is so loud!"

"I know! He does this all the time. He's so embarrassing! I'll see you later. He won't stop calling my name until I go," Jason replies as he climbs down the tree and leaps onto the ground.

"Later, Jay!" Jimmy shouts from above.

"See you later!" Jason yells back as he waves to Jimmy and jogs toward his dad's voice.

My dad always believed in saving time and getting things done "instantly!" So using an industrial size bullhorn to tell his kids to come home was just what he did. It didn't bother my dad in the least that the neighbors would all come out of their house to confirm the police weren't outside pulling someone over. We had only lived there a week and the neighbors had already pegged us as "the crazy family". He was driving me absolutely nuts, and there was no end in sight!

Dad, STOP!" Jason roars as he waves his arms.

"Let's go, Toad! Hurry up, its dinner time!" Larry yells into the bullhorn, pretending to sound like a robot.

"Dad, you're sooo freakin' embarrassing! Everyone is looking at you," Jason vents as he kicks a pinecone lying in the street.

"TOOOOAD... Were you eating snacks? Your face is covered with chocolate. I told you we were eating dinner!" Larry scolds.

"I didn't eat anything. I'm going inside! You're way too annoying!" Jason responds as he scampers away.

Larry yells into the bullhorn with a smile, "Jason, I'm going to call up Jim's mom and ask! If you're telling a lie, even a tiny one, you will be punished!"

Jason opens the door, storms inside, and blurts out with frustration, "Mom, seriously, I can't take it!"

"Sorry, did he find his bullhorn already?" Ellen questions with compassion.

Jason pauses, looks at his mother, and blurts out, "YES! All the neighbors were outside staring at him!"

"Go wash your hands sweetie and get ready for dinner," Ellen directs.

Jason trudges to the bathroom and shakes his head with frustration.

Dashing into the house, Larry carefully sets his toy on the kitchen counter.

"Can you tell me why you needed to use your bullhorn to call him in, Larry? You promised me you wouldn't do that anymore. Would you like your kids to *never* want to be around you in public?" Ellen questions with emotion.

"Oh, stop. They don't listen! Especially Jason! I told him when to be home and he completely ignored me!" Larry replies with frustration.

"Well, I'd be embarrassed too if you called me over with a bullhorn, Larry," Ellen responds with annoyance.

With a confused laugh, Poppy Al yells out, "Hell, let's just eat dinner already. I'm starving!"

JASON'S GRANDPARENTS LEAVE

The powder blue leather suitcases are neatly packed and staged by the front door. Jason's grandparents begin their goodbyes with Larry and Ellen as they lovingly embrace.

"Where's Jason?" Gloria questions.

"Toad, where are you?! Your grandparents are getting ready to leave!" yells Larry.

"Hang on, I'm coming!" Jason shouts with excitement.

Annoyed, Larry responds, "HURRY UP, TOAD!"

"Nanny, we have a surprise for you before you go! Everyone, sit down on the couch," Jason directs from the next room.

"Really?" Gloria whispers to Ellen with curiosity.

Jason walks out of the hallway holding his Fisher-Price cassette player and places it on the coffee table. He slowly pulls a tape out of his pocket and hits the eject button. Proudly inserting the cassette, Jason hits play.

"Eric! Adam! I'm ready!" shouts Jason with exhilaration.

The intro to the song *Gloria*, sung by Laura Branigan, begins to play.

Adam and Eric dart into the room in anticipation of the big performance. Uncontrollably, they start jumping up and down with excitement. Jason waves them over and has a quick huddle with his younger brothers. The pre-rehearsed dance routine dedicated to their *Nanny* Gloria begins.

Jason places both of the boys behind him as his back up dancers. He then pulls out two pairs of sunglasses from his pocket and puts a pair on each of his brothers. He leaps in the front to take the lead as the intro starts.

Passionately, Jason begins to lip-sync the opening lyrics of the song: *"Gloria, you're always on the run now."*

Jason's intensity and confidence grows with each line he sings, *"But you really don't remember, was it something that he said? All the voices in your head, calling Gloria."*

The backup dancing brothers are doing their best to mouth the words, shake their hips, and keep the sunglasses from sliding off their faces. Filled with pride, Nanny Gloria and Ellen stand up and start clapping with huge smiles. Poppy Al grabs his camera and sprints over. He begins snapping photos of his grandchildren like he's covering an exclusive fashion shoot. Larry stands up with a proud grin. All the adults are laughing, clapping, and cheering. Jason absolutely loves being the center of attention! He sashays over to the beat of the song and grabs his grandmother's hand. Jason spins her around like an eight-year-old ballroom dancer. The boys finish performing the entire song and the house erupts like the end of a Bruce Springsteen concert!

"Awww… I loved that! Oh my GOD, you guys are the cutest, EVER! You are all so darn adorable," Nanny proudly declares.

"On that note, we should get going before we hit traffic," reminds Poppy Al as he grabs the suitcase and begins to pack up the car.

Everyone starts to say their goodbyes and slowly transition outside as Al finishes loading the rest of the luggage.

"We always love seeing you guys," Nanny Gloria announces, in a sweet, emotional tone.

"Yes, it's always a fun adventure," Poppy Al responds as he glances over to the large dent on the hood of his Caddy.

Nanny walks up to each boy, kneels down, and reminds him how much she loves him. (Adam, Eric, and then Jason).

"Jason, come over here sweetheart," requests Nanny as she kneels down.

"Yes, Nanny?" Jason replies with curiosity.

Gloria gently grabs Jason's chin, looks him in the eyes, and reinforces, "I love you very much. You know that right?"

"Yes, I know you love me, Nanny," Jason replies, as he stares back with intense eye contact.

"I need you to do Nanny a big favor."

"OK, what?" questions Jason with uncertainty.

Anticipation builds as Nanny Gloria pauses for a few seconds.

"Yes, Nanny?" softly questions Jason again.

"I want you to treat your brother Eric with love and respect, all the time. He's a very, very, sweet little boy, like you all are. You're his older brother and he looks up to you. Eric loves you very much. Can you promise Nanny and Poppy you will do everything you can to be a good big brother, please? It's important," Nanny Gloria reinforces with sincere emotion.

"OK, Nanny. I will," Jason responds quietly.

"I really hope so. It makes us sad when you're not being nice to Eric. I know you will do it. I know you will start to treat him the right way. Listen… Poppy and I have one more gift for you. It is something very special because you are the oldest brother."

Nanny Gloria reaches into her purse and carefully pulls out a mid-1970's CANON 35-millimeter camera.

"This is your grandfather's very first camera. He used this for many years. I know you mentioned you wanted one. This is a real "big boy" gift. I am going to give it to your dad and he can show you how it works. When you're done taking pictures, he can get the film developed for you. Believe it or not, some stores can get it done in only one hour!"

"Wow! Thanks, Nanny! I promise you I will take care of this camera forever!" Jason blurts out with amazement.

"I want you to use it to take as many special pictures of your friends and family that you can. One day, those photos will be treasures and bring you lots of happiness!" Nanny advises as she gives Jason a warm embrace.

"OK, everybody, we love you, but we really do have to hit the road," Nanny informs as she stands up and smiles.

Everyone gives their final hugs and well wishes.

Poppy Al and Nanny Gloria walk to the car, open the doors, and each get in. The boys all run over and start shouting goodbye as they wave to their grandparents with frowns on their faces.

"We love you!" Poppy Al shouts as he rolls down the window.

"Bye, we love you, all!" yells out Nanny Gloria.

Al turns to Gloria and whispers with a smile, "Well, at least we have our dent on the hood to remember this trip."

Gloria looks at Al, smiles, and responds, "Yes, we have the dent," as she kisses him on the cheek.

The Cadillac cautiously pulls out of the driveway as the children across the street throw their baseball. Al promptly hits the gas pedal and speeds away!

Chapter Seven
The Magic Continues

Summer of 1985

T wo high-powered remote-control cars (GRASSHOPPER models) are tearing up the dirt track that Jason and Jimmy built in the vacant lot on the street. The cars battle for victory as the intense race unfolds. The sound of innocent laughter and excitement fills the air.

One remote control car pulls ahead as the other shoots off the dirt ramp and takes the lead. It's like a Saturday afternoon NASCAR race. The excitement rapidly builds. With five seconds left in the intense race, the car leading hits a rock and viciously flips over right before the finish line.

Jason screams out laughing, "YES! I win! I beat you!" Frustrated, Jimmy sprints over and quickly picks up his car.

"You're lucky, Jay! You're SO lucky!" Jimmy declares as the boys high-five and walk down the street.

"Aww, man, I thought I was gonna lose that race. Your car has way better tires than mine," compliments Jason.

"Yeah, like I said, you just got lucky," Jimmy reminds as he starts to run toward his house.

"Where are you going?" yells Jason.

"TREE HOUSE, Let's go!" Jimmy exclaims.

"Wait up! Man… He loves that tree house," Jason mumbles with a smile.

Moments later, Jason enters the side yard and shouts, "JIM!"

"I'm up here!" Jimmy wails out, holding a thick brown rope. He is balancing effortlessly on the highest branch in the tree.

"What the heck are you doing? You're going to fall!" Jason reprimands.

"LOOK OUT BELOW!" Jimmy screams out with exhilaration, as he suddenly leaps off the tree branch doing his best Tarzan impression.

He gracefully swings back onto the first level tree house platform with ease.

Thoroughly impressed, Jason darts up the 2x4's to congratulate his best friend.

Breathing heavily, Jimmy turns on his battery-operated radio and casually sits down on a plastic milk crate.

"That was AWESOME, dude! Ya know, I love living here," Jason announces as he sits down Indian style.

"Living where? In my tree house?" responds Jimmy with laughter.

With sarcasm Jason clarifies, "Real funny, Jim. I meant that I moved onto this street and met you."

"JAAASSSOOON!! JAAASSSOOON!!"

"YOUR DAD!" Jimmy yells as he jumps off the milk crate completely startled.

"JAAASSSOOON!! JAAASSSOOON!!"

"Yup, that's my dad," Jason snickers as he shakes his head.

"DINNNER TIME!! JAAASSSOOON!! JAAASSSOOON!!

"My GOD, how long is he going to do that for?" questions Jimmy with a confused look on his face.

"Until I leave and go home. Maybe I should just stand here and see how long he will yell my name. I've never actually timed him," Jason replies with a loud belly laugh.

"JAAASSSOOON!! DINNNER TIME!!!"

"Dude, you need to go now. I can't listen to this anymore," Jimmy pleads in a serious tone.

He nudges Jason to leave with his elbow.

With laughter, Jason responds, "OK, OK, I won't make you listen to this any longer."

"JAAASSSOOON!! "JAAASSSOOON!!"

With concern, Mrs. Gallo hollers out the window, "Is everything OK, boys? I hear very loud yelling! Is someone hurt?"

"No, sorry, Mrs. G. It's just my dad calling me for dinner. This is what happens when he needs me to come home," Jason explains with embarrassment.

Mrs. G. encourages, "Well you better go, sweetie! It sounds like he's not too happy."

"Yeah, I'm going now. He's not mad. It's just what he does," Jason explains, as he quickly scrambles down the tree and starts to run down the side yard.

"Bye, Jimmy! Bye, Mrs. G! I'll see you later."

"See you later, Jay!" Jimmy shouts out from the top of the tree house.

"Wow! That's one loud man!" Mrs. G. declares as she shakes her head and closes the window.

"Dad, I'm coming!" Jason shrieks out as he turns the corner of Jimmy's side yard.

"Jeez! He is so damn embarrassing!" Jason mutters as he clenches his teeth and speed walks toward his house, looking at the ground.

The surrounding neighbors have now come outside to investigate what all the commotion is.

"Really, Dad? Really? Do you have to yell so loud that the entire block has to hear you call me?" questions Jason with anger and tears in his eyes.

"Don't be fresh, TOAD! If you don't like it you can move out!" yells Larry as Jason runs by him.

As he opens the front door, Jason loudly vents to his mother, "I can't take it! Daddy is ALWAYS embarrassing me!"

Quickly, Jason dashes into his room and slams the door closed.

Larry enters the house moments later.

"Why do you have to do that, Larry?" Ellen questions with frustration.

"Do what? I called him in for dinner," Larry explains.

Ellen shakes her head and walks over to Jason's room. She gently knocks on his door.

"What?!" Jason yells out with anger.

"It's your mother," Ellen delicately responds.

"What is it, Mommy? I want to be alone," Jason replies with sadness.

"Listen, I know your father can be embarrassing sometimes..."

Jason interrupts Ellen in mid-sentence and snaps back with fierce emotion, "SOMETIMES?! Are you kidding me? It's ALL THE TIME!"

With understanding, Ellen replies, "He doesn't mean to be that way. It's just how your father is. He loves you very much. You know, the truth is sometimes people just don't realize the way they act can upset others. They really have no idea. You have to try and not take it personally and just ignore it."

"Eric, get out of my room!" Jason screams as his little brother curiously peers in to see what the discussion is about.

"Hey! That's not nice, Jason. He didn't do anything wrong," Ellen responds.

"Ugh! He drives me crazy, Mommy. He's always making me mad!" Jason explains with frustration.

Eric begins to sob and runs out.

Ellen attempts to explain, "You need to be patient with him, Jason. Life is not always easy. One day you will need Eric. He is a kind little boy. He will always be there for you. So be there for him, please!"

"NEVER! I can't stand him. Just leave me alone!" Jason begs with annoyance.

"You better stay in here and think about what you just said. I'm extremely disappointed in you," Ellen replies as she holds back her tears and walks out.

Jason takes a pillow and folds it over his head. He loudly blurts out, "UGH!!"

Moments later there's another knock on the door. Irritated, Jason questions, "WHAT?! Who's there?"

The door opens slowly. A small adorable face slowly peeks in.

"Jay-Jay?" questions four-year-old Adam as he holds his Chewbacca STAR WARS action figure and casually skips into the room.

"Oh, hey, Bub. What's going on?" responds Jason.

In a squeaky toddler voice, Adam requests, "Hey, don't be mean to Eric!" as he turns around, bends over and loudly passes gas.

Adam looks back and grins. He sticks his tongue out at Jason and then playfully skips out of the room.

Immediately, there's a third knock on the door.

"Oh my GOD, are you serious?" whines Jason.

"TOAD!" Jason pauses and quietly ignores his father.

The door briskly opens and Larry walks in.

Irritated, Jason questions, "What, Dad?"

"What is your problem, Toad? You're always angry!" Larry shouts.

"Adam just farted on me and it smelled really bad," Jason complains, trying not to giggle.

"You 100 percent deserve it!" declares Larry as he laughs hysterically.

"Ugh, you're all driving me crazy. I'm tired, Dad. Please stop," Jason politely requests.

"Listen to me and then I'll leave you alone. You can be upset at your mom and me. We're not perfect. We know that. But the way you treat your brother Eric is terrible."

"Dad, he just drives me nuts," Jason interrupts.

"Please! Shut your mouth and listen to me!" Larry demands. "He loves you and wants to be your buddy. I don't know why you have so much built up anger toward him. You were the only one around for the first three years of your life. I'm sorry if you still wish that was the case, but you got two brothers."

"Yeah, I know, Dad. I can count," interrupts Jason again.

Larry steps closer to Jason and shouts, "LOOK AT ME! I'm serious, Jason. I know it's very hard to imagine at ten years old, but life ain't easy. You're going to have lots of great stuff happen in your life, but you're also gonna have lots of things that don't go your way. You will ALWAYS have your brothers! I want you to make me a promise."

Annoyed, Jason loudly questions, "What, Dad?"

"Jason, I said look at me!" demands Larry with a firm tone.

Whining, Jason repeats, "What, Dad?"

"One day, your brother is going to need you and one day you're going to need your brother. So when that day comes, the outcome will be an accumulation of how you treated each other over the years."

"What does 'accumulation' mean?" Jason enquires with a sincere voice.

"It means how you treated someone over time. Got it?" Larry bluntly explains.

"Yeah, I got it. Jeez, Dad," Jason replies quietly as he stares into his father's dejected eyes.

"Start treating Eric better. He loves you and it makes me sad when you're not nice to him. Think about it, Jason. Make the right choices and decisions," Larry encourages as he walks out of Jason's room and closes the door.

When you're in fifth grade and living in the moment of being a kid, you're not thinking about next month, next week, or even tomorrow. When my father would speak to me about "later in life" and the importance of being kind to my brothers, I just didn't get it. Then again, I wasn't supposed to, I was a kid. To me, my brother Eric was just this annoying little gnat that irritated me, upset me, and... well... I guess sometimes made me laugh. (chuckling) I truly believe it hurt my dad when I would mistreat Eric. You see, my father didn't talk about it often, almost never, but as far back as I could remember, I always had a hunch that the reason he was so sensitive about how I treated my brothers, was because of how poorly he treated his. I truly believe deep inside, a part of him really regretted that. It's unfortunate that he was never able to be honest and just share his shortcomings. I think sometimes as parents, we try and teach our children to do the "right thing", but don't always have the courage to tell them that we made the exact same mistakes.

Chapter Eight

The Ultimate Water Balloon Fight

Like a heat seeking missile, a water balloon shoots through the air and bursts directly on the center of Jason's back.

"I got you!" Jimmy blurts out and then darts away in the opposite direction.

"Your ass is grass and I'm the lawn mower!" yells Jason with echoing laughter.

He reaches deep into the bucket and grabs a fresh, plump water balloon. The sound of scampering and heavy breathing is heard as Jason chases Jimmy down the side yard of his house.

"Get over here, punk! Where are you?" Jason roars with a smile of pure joy.

Unable to see or locate Jimmy, Jason cautiously pauses. He stops and begins to carefully search his backyard. Peering behind bushes and trees Jason comes up empty handed.

"JIMMY?!" Jason yells out with the anticipation of a response.

With no answer, Jason hesitantly walks toward the playground. He sees the empty swings briskly swaying back and forth.

Jason yells out again, "Dude, if you're hiding, I'm gonna get ya! I'm warning you. You better be ready!"

Unexpectedly, whimpering is heard on the opposite side of the swing set. "Jimmy? Is that you?" Jason shouts with concern.

"OUCH, HELP!"

Out of the corner of his eye, Jason notices his friend lying on the ground. Jimmy is clutching his leg as he rolls around with a grimace of pain on his face.

Jason darts over as fast as he can to investigate what happened.

"Damn, my leg!" Jimmy yelps as he continues to cringe in pain.

"Are you OK? Do you need me to call your mom to come get you?" questions Jason with deep concern.

"I don't know, but my arm is killing me!" responds Jimmy with a subtle grin.

"Hang on! I'm going to get an ice pack!" Jason shouts as he takes off and then quickly stops short in his tracks.

"WAIT, you said your leg was hurt. Now it's your arm?" Jason questions with confusion.

"I mean, my leg is killing me!" Jimmy confirms as he moans in pain and starts laughing.

Perplexed, Jason bends down to extend his hand and help lift Jimmy up off the ground.

With success, Jimmy rises up and screams, "GOT YOU!" He pegs Jason with another water balloon right in the chest.

Jimmy quickly gains his balance, spins around Jason, and attempts to run back down the side of the house.

"That's it!" Jason mumbles to himself as he abruptly stops in his tracks.

He pauses and takes aim. Like an NFL quarterback, Jason cocks his arm back and then releases the water balloon like it was shot out of a rocket launcher... BULLSEYE! Jimmy is hit square in the leg.

"FINALLY! I got you! Whoo Hooo!" Jason screams out with immense joy while leaping in the air.

Jimmy tries desperately to keep his balance, before sliding headfirst into the grass.

Quickly, Jason dashes over to the scene.

"Damn, Jay! Look what you did!" Jimmy responds as he shows Jason the bright red welt pulsating on his leg.

"Now my leg really hurts," confirms Jimmy with sarcastic laughter.

"Well, that's what you get for messing with me," Jason proudly jokes.

Both boys begin to walk toward the side of the house, when they suddenly hear the thundering sound of airbrakes popping close by.

"What the hell is that?" Jason asks in confusion.

Jimmy shouts with excitement, "Let's go check it out!"

"OK, let's go!" responds Jason with eagerness as the boys dart down the side of the house toward the closed wooden gate.

Frustrated, Jason screams out, "The gate won't open! It's stuck!"

"Dude, hurry up! Let's go!" Jimmy responds bouncing with excitement.

Impatient, Jason shouts, "I'm trying, but it's completely jammed. It won't budge."

Without warning, Jimmy leaps in the air and frantically attempts to scale the wooden gate. He pulls down on the top of the gate for leverage as the plank of wood rips right off the nails.

Airborne, with arms flailing, Jimmy slams to the ground as the wooden plank lands right next to him.

"Oh damn! I'm going to be in HUGE trouble! My dad's going to kill me. He just had that fence built!" Jason screams out with anxiety.

Swiftly, Jason picks up the plank of wood. In a scramble, he pushes the cracked plank back into the nails, *upside down.*

Just as Jimmy gets up and scurries to wipe the dirt off his knees, Jason successfully jars open the gate.

Instantaneously, Jimmy dashes through the opening.

"Jim! STOP! What's going on? Why are you in such a rush?" Jason shouts.

Jimmy pauses and quickly turns around with his arms in the air.

With surprise he questions, "You REALLY don't know what that sound means?!"

"I have no idea, dude!" replies Jason with confusion.

Elated, Jimmy informs, "MOVING TRUCK!"

"Huh?" responds Jason.

"Jay! That sound, it was the same one I heard the morning you moved in. It's a moving truck that just parked! How don't you know that? Someone is moving in! We need to go see who it is. Come on!" Jimmy directs as he darts away with anticipation.

"Look down there! Let's go!" Jimmy points with eagerness as he glances back at Jason.

Both boys scamper toward the sound of the idling engine. With their hands on their hips, panting like dogs, Jason and Jimmy cautiously approach the moving truck.

Out of breath, Jason questions with curiosity, "I wonder who moved in."

"I don't know, but I need water. I'm dying of thirst!" Jimmy informs as he briskly walks toward the outside faucet.

With a loud whisper, Jason cautions, "What the hell are you doing, dude? We don't even know who lives here!"

Jimmy waves Jason over as he nervously turns on the faucet. He bends down and starts slurping the water like an overheated dog.

"Um, excuse me. Can I help you?" questions an adult male voice from an opened house window.

Startled, Jimmy frantically turns the faucet off and sprints back towards Jason.

The front door slowly creeks open as Jason and Jimmy both cautiously pause. With anticipation, they shuffle over to see who is walking out of the house.

Suddenly, a young boy on roller skates, wearing scuffed up knee pads and a hockey helmet, zooms out of the doorway. He continues to gain speed as he shoots down the steep driveway, trying to maintain his balance. With his arms flailing, the boy zips past Jason and Jimmy as he heads toward the street going full speed.

In the distance, there's a car heading down the street. The unknown boy continues to accelerate as he quickly approaches the road. Jimmy sees the car out of the corner of his eye and takes off like a cheetah. He tries to get the mysterious roller skaters attention as the car is rapidly getting closer.

"HEY! STOP!" shrieks Jimmy at the top of his lungs as the car continues barreling down the street.

Bravely, Jimmy dashes into the road, franticly waving his arms for the car to stop. Just as the boy flies in front of the car, the driver desperately slams the brakes. The car uncontrollably skids as smoke bellows from the tires. The smell of burnt rubber immediately fills the air as the car thrusts forward and then abruptly stops.

"Holy shit! Are you OK?!" wails Jimmy.

The neighbors become spectators and quickly flock outside to investigate what happened.

The car is quickly placed in park as a teenage girl leaps out of the driver's side door hysterically crying.

She franticly sprints over to the freckle-faced boy and yells out, "Damn it! Are you OK?"

The front of the car is gently resting against the unharmed boy.

"What the fuck were you thinking?!" the girl screams out with emotion. Tears are streaming down her face as she repeatedly pushes the boy's shoulder.

With frustration, Jimmy screams out, "My sister almost killed you!"

The passenger door slowly opens. A massive leg extends out of the car, followed by an even larger body. A man with a thick black mustache, military style tinted sunglasses, and the look of a former marine exits the car.

The man questions with anger, "What the hell is wrong with you, kid? We almost ran your ass over!"

"Dad, calm down!" pleads Jimmy.

In shock, the boy looks around dazed and suddenly freezes. With an awkward smile he announces loudly, "Hello, I'm Bobby!"

"Well, you're not very smart, BOBBY!" Mr. Gallo angrily declares.

"Dad, STOP!" shouts Jimmy.

"Get in the car, Kathy, NOW!" Mr. Gallo demands.

"That kid is an absolute idiot!" Jimmy's father mumbles as he gets in the Buick, slams the door, and drives away.

"Well... I guess that's your official welcome to our street," Jimmy sarcastically blurts out.

"Thanks, your dad is one scary man!" replies Bobby as he wipes the immense amount of sweat off his forehead.

"Yeah I know. He was in a good mood, if you can actually believe that," responds Jimmy with a nervous grin.

"A good mood?" questions Bobby with surprise.

"Yup, my older sister just got her license, so dad won't have to drive her around anymore," Jimmy informs.

"Sweet, maybe she can drop us off at the arcade. I saw there's an ALADDIN'S CASTLE at the Countryside Mall. You know, I actually have the high score on SPY HUNTER," Bobby declares with an irritating snort-laugh.

Jimmy and Jason stare at each other as they shake their heads in disbelief of the obnoxious laugh.

"So, where did you come from? I mean, move from?" Jason shouts out.

"We moved from Ohio! My dad's company transferred him here," Bobby responds.

With pride and excitement, Jason questions, "Ohio? That's awesome! My dad went to Ohio State. He's always talking about some guys named Woody and Archie. I think they may have been his roommates or something."

Curious, Bobby questions, "So, are there a lot of kids that live on this street?"

"Yeah, there's lot of kids around, but me and Jay are definitely the coolest," Jimmy chuckles.

"JAAASSSOOON!! JAAASSSOOON!!"

"WHOA, what's that?" questions Bobby with concern as he braces himself.

Jimmy and Jason laugh as they wink at each other in acknowledgment of the nightly name-calling humor.

"JAAASSSOOON!!"

"I think you better go, Jay. Meet me at the tree!" Jimmy instructs with a smile.

Jason begins jogging backwards and yells out, "That's my dad! You'll get to know him, trust me!"

Turning around, Jason walks toward his house grinning. In the distance he sees his father's arms flapping like a bird. Larry is hysterical!

"WHAT THE HELL HAPPENED TO MY GATE?! And don't even try and blame this one on your brother Eric!" shouts Larry in disbelief.

With a straight face Jason responds, "Huh, I'm not really sure what you're talking about, big guy!"

"I just spent thousands of dollars on that fence! You lost your ATARI for a month. I'm NOT kidding!" Larry confirms.

"OK, Big L. ATARI is old school anyway," responds Jason as he takes his finger and pokes the side of his dad's plump belly.

"Jason, do you see me laughing? You're gonna be punished for not treating my property with respect!" Larry threatens.

"OK, big guy, I'm sorry. Take it out of my allowance!" Jason yells out as he jogs around his father for several minutes trying to induce laughter.

Larry responds, "Toad, when you come home later, you're in big trouble! TRUST ME!"

"OK, Chubs! I love you," Jason says with sincerity as he jogs away and blows his dad a kiss.

Larry shakes his head and struggles to fight the urge to laugh.

The glowing summer sun is beginning to set as Jason skips down the street toward Jimmy's house. He eagerly approaches the tree house.

Toward the top of the tree, Jason hears shuffling as the branches sway back and forth. He quickly looks up and sees Bobby casually sitting on Jimmy's "private" tree house seat.

"Hey! Bobby! What the heck are you doing? You're not allowed up there. That's off limits. NO ONE is allowed on that seat except Jimmy! Get down, now!" Jason orders with a scowl.

Bobby stands up on the seat and grabs a tree branch with each hand. He slowly shakes his hips side to side mocking Jason. Concurrently, Jimmy walks out of the patio screen door, drinking a CAPRI-SUN and holding a FRUIT ROLL-UP.

Completely disheveled, Jason dashes over to report the severe tree house violation.

Flustered, Jason yells out, "You won't believe what's going on! This new kid Bobby is sitting on your seat! I told him to get off and he won't listen!"

"Yeah, I know," nonchalantly replies Jimmy as he peels his FRUIT ROLL-UP off the plastic backing.

"Ya know what?" questions Jason completely dumbfounded.

"I know," Jimmy casually repeats.

"You know what?" Jason questions again, beginning to get agitated.

"I told him he could sit up there," Jimmy confirms as he chomps on his snack.

"WAIT, WHAT? You told him he could sit up there? Are you freaking kidding me? So, let me get this straight. I've known you for two years, *two years*, and you NEVER let anyone sit in that seat! This new kid you've known for only two hours, *two hours* and he gets your permission *like that*?" Jason quizzes as he snaps his fingers.

Jimmy and Jason stare into each other's eyes, trying to figure out the next words to be said.

Suddenly, one tear trickles out of the corner of Jason's eye. Heartbroken, he looks up at the top of the tree and sees Bobby still standing on the seat. He obnoxiously sticks out his tongue at Jason and grins.

Unexpectedly, Jason dashes down the side of the house.

"Jay, where are you going?!" shouts Jimmy as he attempts to chase after Jason.

Moments later, Jimmy approaches the front yard and notices Jason slouched over. He's sitting on the sewer in front of the house, with his head hanging low in defeat.

"Jay, what's a matter?" Jimmy questions.

Jason looks up. His eyes are red and glossy. He adamantly replies, "NOTHING!"

"Why are you so upset? What happened?" Jimmy wonders with concern.

Jason loudly snaps back at Jimmy and points to the tree, "What happened? THAT HAPPENED!

"Oh, that? I just felt bad for him. My sister almost flattened the new kid. When Bobby asked if he could sit on my seat, I told him he could. I'm really sorry, Jay. You should have been the first person other than me to sit up there. You're my best friend. You know that," Jimmy genuinely reinforces.

Inconspicuously, Jimmy slowly proceeds to stick his finger in his mouth. Without warning, he inserts it deep inside Jason's ear and administers a massive WET WILLY!

"Dude, you are so DISGUSTING!" yells Jason as he quickly springs up laughing.

While struggling to wipe his ear, Jason blurts out, "That's it, revenge time! You must pay the price for what you've done and face my wrath!"

Jason dives toward Jimmy and tackles his legs. The boys fall to the ground as they playfully wrestle. The sound of joyful laughter and innocent name calling can be heard.

> When you're in the moment, sometimes it's hard to understand or realize how special it really is. How magical life can be. How simple things like wrestling with your best friend brings so much joy. Why do we over complicate life as we grow older? Why does the search for happiness become a full-time job, an obsession? Is it a newly remodeled kitchen? Is it the latest model luxury SUV? Is it the next executive position at the office? Maybe, just maybe...if we stop, close our eyes, and take a deep breath we can remember the essence and simplicity of our childhood – what true happiness really is. Connections, relationships, friendships, disagreements, handshakes, hugs, laughter and tears. Not through a "TEXT" or a "LIKE", but by a genuine physical interaction. Maybe, just maybe...

Chapter Nine
Jason Signs a Contract

Toooaaaadd!! Toooaaddd!!"

Abruptly, Jason is awakened by the intense, piercing sound of his father's voice. His eyes pop wide open and he springs out of his bed. Jason glances at the digital clock that displays that it's 6:30 a.m. He proceeds to exit his room and sees his dad sitting down with a manila folder lying on the kitchen table.

"Toad, sit down!" Larry orders.

Jason questions, "What Dad? Its 6:30 in the morning and its Saturday. What's going on?"

"My fence! That's what's going on. I have something we need to go over," informs Larry as he puts on his reading glasses.

Exhausted, Jason questions, "OK, what is it, Dad?"

Larry slowly opens the top-secret folder while Jason tries to peer at the contents inside.

"Fence restitution? What the heck does that mean, Dad?" asks Jason as he pronounces 'restitution' incorrectly.

"It means that you are going to pay me back every penny for the gate that you broke," confirms Larry.

Jason glares at his father with confusion, "Huh? How? And what's all of that writing on the paper?"

With conviction, Larry clarifies, "It's a contract that I drew up. I'm going to read it to you so you understand what it means. Ya ready?"

Irritated, Jason shakes his head and whines, "Fine, I'm tired, Dad. Hurry up, please! I just want to go back to sleep already!"

Professionally, Larry begins to recite the detailed contract as if he worked in a law office.

JULY 15TH 1985

I, Jason Todd Shapiro hereby agree to the following terms and conditions of this contract.

I will be assigned extra chores around the house to earn additional allowance. Each week on Saturday, Larry Shapiro will give me the money I earned and I will hand it right back to him.

Any money I receive as gifts from my grandparents or relatives will also go toward the repair of the gate until it is paid for.

Failure to complete my assigned chores will result in me being grounded.

Sign: Jason Shapiro _____
Larry Shapiro _____

"DAD? What the heck is this? You're making me sign a contract? I'm only ten years old. I'm a kid! We break things. That's what we do," Jason desperately attempts to reason.

Annoyed, Larry responds, "That's fine Toad, but you're going to pay me back. EVERY PENNY! Got it?"

"Larry, what's going on?" yells Ellen as she tries to keep her voice to a very intense whisper. "The kids are sleeping! What is wrong with you?!"

"Mommy!" Jason yelps as he runs over and hugs Ellen's legs. "He's making me sign a contract and he's taking ALL my money!"

Confused, Ellen questions, "What are you talking about? Larry, STOP with the stupid contracts already! You promised me you would cut that out after you did it to my brother when he accidently scratched my car. It's a ridiculous thing and it makes people feel uncomfortable. So, stop it already!"

Adamantly, Larry responds, "No, Ellen, I'm not going to stop! The gate is broken. He needs to learn there are consequences to his actions."

Jason's infant brother Jared begins to cry in his crib. Ellen puts her finger in the air and demands quiet. She glares at Larry with eyes so piercing they could shoot laser beams.

"You just woke the baby! What is wrong with you?! We are going to have a serious talk later about this ridiculous way of teaching your ten-year-old son a "life lesson". I have to go get the baby that YOU just woke up!" Ellen scolds.

Jason stares at his father as he hesitantly picks up the pen and reluctantly signs the document. Jason lowers his head down and mopes back to his room. He flings the door closed and leaps back into his bed. Moments later, a soft knock is heard on Jason's bedroom door.

"WHAT DAD?!" questions Jason.

Another knock follows.

"What do you want, Dad?" Jason asks again with frustration.

The door slowly creaks open and a little head peers in.

"Oh, it's you, Eric. What do you want?" Jason responds with disappointment.

Eric hops over, imitating a bunny rabbit as he jumps onto Jason's bed. He lies down and puts his head on Jason's chest.

Looking at Jason in the eyes, Eric states with sincere emotion, "I love you."

"OK, OK, thanks, Berry," Jason uncomfortably replies.

"Do you love me?" questions Eric with uncertainty.

Ellen walks over to the slightly opened door. She is holding Jason's baby brother and proceeds to quietly observe the genuine interaction of the two boys.

Eric stands up and begins feverishly jumping as he repeats "Do you love me?" several times in a row.

Suddenly, Eric pauses as he looks Jason in the eyes again and confidently waits for his older brother's response.

Annoyed, Jason pauses and replies, "Eric, please get out of my room. I'm not in a good mood."

The look of disappointment is seen on Ellen's face as she steps back from the door.

Defeated, Eric slides off the bed and begins to walk out of the room with tears in his eyes.

Ellen takes another step back as Eric exits the room. Jason stands up and walks over to his closet. He begins to get dressed for the day.

Ellen enters the room shaking her head in disappointment as she approaches Jason.

"Hi, what's going on?" she tenderly questions.

Startled, Jason responds, "Oh, hey, Mom. You scared me. I didn't see you there."

"I've been here the whole time, Jason. He loves you very much. He looks up to you. You're his big brother," Ellen reminds Jason as her eyes begin to well. She slowly wipes away her tears with one hand while holding the giggling baby in the other.

"I'm sorry, but you have brothers. Eric is a special little boy. You all are, but you break his spirit when you don't give him back the love he gives you. Do you understand that?" Ellen questions with emotion.

"What does 'break his spirit' mean?" asks Jason.

Struggling to reply, Ellen pushes out her response, "It means that a person believes in something with all their heart and then finds out it isn't true. I have to go, Jason. Please, think about what I said. Your grandparents and uncle are coming today. Finish getting ready and I'll go make you breakfast."

Once dressed, Jason moseys over to the kitchen table. He glances over as Larry and his younger brother Adam are each sitting on a wicker back chair at the kitchen bar. They're both wearing matching navy fleece bathrobes. Larry is reading the weekly edition of the TV GUIDE as Adam is inspecting Jason's copy of SUPERFUDGE. He is mimicking his dad's every move with admiration.

Jason plops down at the kitchen table and begins to munch on his bowl of LUCKY CHARMS.

"What are you doing today, Toad?" loudly questions Larry.

Adam attempts to imitate his father, "Yeah, what are you doing today?"

"Shush, Bub, keep your voice down," loudly instructs Larry.

"Um, I don't know. Probably going over to Jim's in a little bit," responds Jason.

With exhilaration, Larry responds, "Just be home by noon, Toad. Your grandparents, my brother, AND his new girlfriend are coming over today!"

"Girlfriend?" Adam playfully questions as he starts to uncontrollably giggle.

"Listen, you guys better behave! I'm telling you both, there better be no arguing or fighting while they're here. Got it?!" Larry shouts.

"Yeah! You better behave," Adam snickers.

Tired, Jason responds, "Please don't be annoying, Bub."

"I gotta get out of here," Jason mumbles to himself as he gets up.

Just as he begins to walk away, Jason pauses and glances at the cereal box.

He announces, "Oh yeah! I totally forgot to take the prize out."

Jason walks back over and slowly inserts his arm deep into the cereal box. He begins to feverishly search for the hidden treasure as cereal trickles out of the box and covers the floor.

Finally, Jason yanks out the hidden gem like he was pulling a fish from a lake.

In victory, Jason proudly yells out, "YES, I GOT IT!"

"Whatcha get?" Adam questions as he spins around in his chair with excitement.

"I don't know, some kind of treasure box," Jason responds with curiosity.

Adam says with anticipation, "So, open it! What are you waiting for?"

Without any hesitation, Jason quickly tears apart the clear wrapping and slowly opens the small plastic toy. Surprised, he sees a hidden message inside.

Jason unfolds the secret note and begins to read it to himself, *"There's no buddy like a brother."*

He intently stares at the message and then looks at Eric as he walks by.

With disappointment, Adam shouts back, "Well, that's a stupid prize! It's terrible!"

Jason carefully folds the message back up and puts the paper in his pocket.

"Hey, Dad, I'm going over to Jimmy's," Jason informs.

"Be back on time!" Larry mumbles as he devours his plate full of mouthwatering bacon.

Filled with eagerness to start his day, Jason opens the front door and dashes out of the house.

It's a magnificent Saturday morning. The sky is filled with beaming rays from the warm bright sun. Children are beginning to skip outside to explore the adventures of the day. Multiple garage doors are opening as the neighborhood kids begin to ride their bikes and play tag. Jason is walking down the sidewalk as the early morning summer breeze blows directly on his face. He pauses and smiles with pure contentment as he soaks up the euphoric atmosphere.

As Jason approaches Jimmy's house, he notices Mr. Gallo walking to his car and opening the trunk with his key. He proceeds to pull out a Toys R Us bag and then charges back inside his house. Jason instantly increases his speed to a light jog. His eyes are filled with uncontrolled curiosity.

"What's in that bag?" Jason wonders to himself aloud.

He arrives at the Gallo's front door and begins to intently knock with no answer. After several minutes, Jason rings the doorbell and patiently waits while tapping his foot. Another minute passes. Finally, Jimmy's older sister Kathy answers the door. She looks like she just rolled out of bed from a house party the night before. Clearly hung over, Kathy begins to intently stare into space. Unsure how to respond, Jason stares back with a smirk. Suddenly, he ducks under Kathy's arm as she props the front door open. He proceeds cautiously as he enters the house.

The sound of laughing and cheering is immediately heard echoing from the family room. As Jason walks closer, he hears the most phenomenal theme song known to mankind. SUPER MARIO BROTHERS!

Puzzled, Jason eagerly walks closer toward the clapping and giggling. He pauses and looks at the TV screen in awe. Jason can't contain his emotions any longer.

He places both hands on his cheeks and screams out with joy, "OH MY GOD! You got a NINTENDO! OH MY GOD! OH MY GOD!"

Startled, Jimmy turns around and sprints toward Jason. The two boys immediately embrace. They begin leaping up and down as if they had just won a shopping spree at Toys R Us.

"I CAN'T BELIEVE IT!" Jason blurts out as he promptly sits down on the floor.

He begins to admire the little grey box as if it were the greatest invention the world had ever seen.

Suddenly, out of the corner of his eye, Jason spots the "Holy Grail", the NINTENDO ENTERTAINMENT SYSTEM ZAPPER! Cautiously, Jason scoops it up with two hands as if he was in possession of the sacred Torah. His hands are trembling as he carefully holds the treasure steady.

"Hi, honey," Mrs. Gallo welcomes Jason with her usual sincere sweet tone.

"I'm telling you boys, you better not think you're going to be playing that "thing" all summer long," Mrs. Gallo mentions as she chuckles.

"Ma, that's so silly. We wouldn't do that. Come on! We're only gonna play it every single minute, of every single hour, of every single day!" yells out Jimmy in hysterics.

Jason and Jimmy embrace again and begin bouncing up and down simultaneously.

"JIMMY!" the rumbling militant voice pierces through the house. You better shut your mouth, son, and listen to your mother or that "game box" will end up in a cardboard box!"

Flustered, Jimmy responds "OK, I got it!"

Cautiously, Jason whispers, "Man, your dad is scary! I guess mine isn't that bad after all!"

"I know, he sounds like Sargent Slaughter," replies Jimmy with a smirk.

Mrs. Gallo overhears Jason and Jimmy's conversation and responds, "Boys, listen, both of your fathers love you dearly. Being a parent is a tough job. They both do the best they can. When you're older you will realize that. They just want you to be respectful, kind, hardworking young men one day. Life's not easy. I know when you're young you can't really understand that. Everything your fathers do is to try and prepare you for the future." There is a short pause. "Do you want a snack? You boys look really hungry. What can I get you? How does a cookie and some Kool-Aid sound?"

"YES, PLEASE!" both boys reply in unison with a "Kool-Aid" smile!"

Mrs. Gallo was probably one of the sweetest women I ever had the privilege of knowing. Her caring and compassionate words were almost soothing to the soul. She was always the voice of reason, even during the most chaotic times. Her perspective always came from the heart. The ability to accept people whole-heartedly for who they are is a very unique gift. Mrs. Gallo did just that.

I've always believed the reason some people feel the need to criticize others, is because they are searching for their own happiness. Subconsciously, they just haven't found it yet. When you have joy in your life, you're too busy investing in yourself, family, and friends to focus on what others are saying or doing. Mrs. Gallo is a reminder that it is possible to JUST BE...

"Holy crap, I gotta go! I totally forgot my uncle and my grandparents are coming over today. My dad is gonna make me sign a contract to not be late if I don't get out of here!"

"Huh?" responds Jimmy with a confused tone.

"I'll tell you about it another time. Bye Mrs. G., thanks for having me over. See ya later!"

Jason scampers down the dark hallway toward the front door. He leaps over Jimmy's older sister, who is now sleeping on the cold, tiled floor. Jason pauses and quickly dashes into Jimmy's room. He grabs the DUKES OF HAZZARD pillow off the bed and then smirks at the Alyssa Milano wall poster on his way out. He proceeds to gently slide the pillow under Kathy's head. Once done, Jason darts outside through the open front door and begins to casually stroll back toward his house.

> So, let me quickly tell you about how I remember my
> dad's parents. They were both very delightful people.
> My Poppy Max absolutely loved the color white. I
> mean, like how Johnny Cash was the man in black,
> Max Shapiro was the man in white. White shoes, white
> socks, white pants, white belt, white button up short
> sleeve shirt, and white hair. (Aqua-netted like no one's
> business!) I mean, a tornado couldn't blow a hair out
> of place! Hell, he even had a white hearing aid. The
> only thing not white, were his thick black frames on his
> glasses. He didn't say much, other than loudly call out
> our names and extend his arms like a zombie so he
> could pinch our cheeks.
>
> Then, there was my Nanny Rhoda. She ran the show,
> and was the only one that could put my dad in his
> place. It was SO damn satisfying to listen to!

Upon entering through the front door, Jason immediately hears his grandmother in action.

"Larry, come outside NOW and talk to us! We haven't seen you in months!" Rhoda yells from outside the open kitchen window.

Everyone has now congregated onto the patio and is kibitzing up a storm.

"Aww, come on, Ma! I got stuff to do inside the house, alright? STOP," Larry groans with frustration.

Rhoda repeats again, "Get out here, NOW!"

"OK, OK, I'm coming," Larry whines.

With pure satisfaction, Jason grins from ear to ear as his father is reprimanded by Nanny Rhoda for not listening.

When Nanny Rhoda wasn't putting my dad in his place, she could also be found repeating every sentence my brothers and I would say, back to my grandfather Max.

(Rhoda recites)

"Max, turn up your hearing aid already!"

"Eric asked you how the drive over was."

"Max, Jason is asking if you thought he got taller!"

"Jesus, Max, Adam wants to know if you got him a toy!"

My grandfather didn't hear a thing. He would just sit there quietly with a huge grin and simply nod every time we asked him a question. We knew he had no clue what was being said, but he looked happy and that's all that really mattered.

And... There's my Uncle Richie! His signature full head of messy brown hair and a mustache thick as a piece of carpet always made me smile.

He was the complete opposite of my father in every way, calm, relaxed, and at peace. The truth is, sometimes I wasn't even sure if they were really related. Everything that bothered and agitated my dad seemed to not even faze my uncle in the least. It's hard to believe that two brothers from the same set of parents could react so differently to the exact same situations.

With a heavy Long Island accent, Richie yells out, "Hey, Jason! I'll be right back in! Hang on! I need to go grab the chaise lounge I brought into the backyard earlier!"

Larry notices his younger brother trying to prop the patio-screen door open with his foot and bring in the large piece of furniture at the same time.

Like a gazelle, Larry darts over boiling with anxiety.

"Rich! Come on! You're gonna rip my screen door! What are you doing?"

Nanny Rhoda follows suit. She pops up out of her chair and shouts out, "Richard! Would ya be careful? What the hell are ya doin'?"

Jason chuckles as the commotion rapidly builds regarding the simple task of bringing in a chaise lounge from the backyard.

Max is still smiling, oblivious to the chaos going on around him.

Without warning, Richie jolts to the left and the chaise lounge causes a small tear in the screen door.

Ballistic, with his arms flapping, Larry has the same reaction as someone dropping his vintage 1967 GIBSON ES-335 electric guitar.

Bolting out of the house with massive concern, Ellen questions, "Is everyone all right?"

"Would you look at what happened!?" Larry roars as he takes both hands and adamantly points at the minor damage in the screen.

"Hey, Larry, is everything OK over there?" shouts Bruce (the neighbor), from his window.

All the Shapiro boys come flocking out of the house to see what the ruckus is about.

The screen tearing incident has now turned into a full-blown circus. Everyone is darting over to inspect the small tear in the screen door. Poppy Max is now sleeping amongst all the crazy commotion.

Uncle Richie somehow sneaks away from the hostile crowd and calls Jason over, "Come with me. I got someone I want you to meet."

They both stroll inside. A young woman with a full head of jet-black curly hair walks over and greets Jason.

Chewing gum, with a heavy New Jersey accent, the woman shouts, "Hey, how are ya?"

"This is Liz, my girlfriend. Liz... This is the guy that made me an uncle," Richie proudly informs as he puts his arm around Jason.

"How ya doin?" Liz questions with a smile.

"Um, good," Jason cautiously responds.

"We got you and your brothers somethin'! Do you wanna see what it is?" she asks.

"Yeah, sure, hold on! I'll be right back!" Jason replies with elation as he dashes away.

Without warning, Liz clutches Uncle Richie's shirt and yanks him into the corner of the family room. Extremely irritated, she whispers, "Richard, I gotta get out of here!"

Surprised, Uncle Richie responds, "Why? What's going on?"

With frustration, Liz responds, "First of all, what the hell is going on outside? It looks like a damn crime scene."

"Aw, that's no big deal. That's just my big brotha. This is all normal stuff," Richie clarifies with a smile.

Annoyed, Liz responds, "Well, your father is sleeping and your mother is screaming for you. The worst part... You ready for this one? I could absolutely puke just telling you. Follow me!

Liz pulls Richie to the bathroom by his arm and points to the ground.

"Someone showered and got water all over the floor?" Jason's uncle questions with confusion.

Disgusted, Liz promptly corrects him, "No, it's gawdamn puddles of urine. I stepped right in it! These boys pissed all over the toilet and the floor. This place is like a zoo full of little animals!"

Suddenly, Liz and Richie quickly turn around as they hear giggling behind them.

All three boys are standing in the doorway with identical smiles.

"Hi, I'm back. I told my brothers that you have presents for us. Oh, and by the way, it was Bub that peed all over the floor," Jason clarifies.

Adam politely waves with a huge innocent grin.

Repulsed, Liz replies, "I gotta get out of here! I'll be in the car, Richard."

With a calm tone, Uncle Richie responds, "OK. Boys, follow me. Single file line, please!" he shouts out with a salute.

The boys accompany their uncle into the guest room beaming with anticipation.

"HALT!" Uncle Richie orders as he puts up his hand and extends his arm. OK, now close your eyes and only open them when I tell you too."

Quietly, Jason's uncle opens up the closet and drags over a massive Toys R Us bag.

"So, there's one big gift to share and then three little ones," Uncle Richie clarifies with a smile.

Discretely, he lifts up the bag and places it in front of the boys.

"OK, you can look now!" Richie announces as he grins with anticipation.

Like a religious experience, the boys lay eyes on the box that contains the most treasured toy in the history of toys!

The Shapiro brothers just received their very own, NINTENDO ENTERTAINMENT SYSTEM!

Screeching, the boy's respond in unison, "This is awesome!"

They begin to uncontrollably hug one another as they jump up and down.

"We got you each one game," Uncle Richie informs the boys as he hands out three separate bags.

Jason opens the first one and shouts out with excitement, "GHOSTS AND GOBLINS? This is the best day of my entire life!"

Like a kid in the candy store, Eric opens the next game and drops to his knees, "CASTLEVANIA? YAY!!"

Last but not least, Adam opens his bag, does a shimmy, and cheers, "SUPER MARIO BROTHERS!"

Jason replies, "SUPER MARIO BROTHERS? Well, we are the Super Shapiro Brothers!"

The boys begin to dance around the room, struggling to restrain their intense excitement. Showing their gratitude, the brothers all run over and tackle their Uncle Richie!

"HEY! What's the commotion about in here?" Larry loudly shouts as he quickly barges into the room.

"Nothing, Larry, relax. I just gave them their presents," Uncle Richie calmly explains.

"Rich, are you kidding me? You got them a NINTENDO without consulting me first?" Larry asks with irritation.

"There's nothing to consult about. It's a video game system, not a car," Richard calmly states as he exits the room.

Chuckling, Uncle Richie overhears Larry tell the boys they will need to sign a contract with play time restrictions.

Jason darts out of the room chasing his uncle and yells out, "Hey, Uncle Richie!"

"Yeah, buddy?" Richie questions.

Grateful, Jason replies, "Thank you! This means a lot to us. I'm so glad you're our uncle."

"Well, I'm glad you're my nephew," Uncle Richie validates.

Jason imagines with excitement, "I was thinking... Maybe one day I'll live by you when I'm older."

"Well, New Jersey is a long way from Florida, but ya never know. We do have snowballs, sleds, and huge colorful leaves that fall from the trees," Uncle Richie describes.

"Wow! That sounds so cool," Jason responds in awe.

"Hey, let's go check on your dad. I think I may need to write him a check for a new screen door," Uncle Richie giggles as he shakes his head.

Jason high-fives his uncle as they walk out to the patio.

"Mr. Jason, come and talk to me ma boy. What's new?" Nanny Rhoda questions with a smile and her arms extended.

"Oh, not much, Nanny, I just hang out with my friends," Jason nonchalantly responds.

Curious, Nanny questions, "Well, do you have one friend that you like the most?"

"Well, yeah, my best friend, Jimmy! We are pretty much like brothers."

"Why is that?" Nanny inquires.

Jason looks Nanny in the eyes and responds, "Well, Nanny, have you ever met someone and you feel like you have known them your entire life? I can't really explain it, but we just kinda clicked. Actually, living on this street also just kinda clicked. It really felt like home from the first day we drove down this street. You know, daddy actually let me go swimming in the pool while our house was still under construction."

Laughing, Jason's grandmother replies, "I'm not surprised your father did that. It really makes Nanny smile that you're so happy living here. Enjoy these times, honey. They will be wonderful memories that you will carry with you for the rest of your life. One day, you may even share all these fun stories with your own kids." Jason chuckles. "I know that's hard to imagine. You're going to think back and remember this house, this beautiful street, and of course all your wonderful friends. You know, even Nanny likes to think back to when I was a little girl."

Surprised, Jason questions, "You were little?"

"Oh, so you're a jokester, are ya?" replies Nanny as she gently pokes Jason in the belly.

"Of course, I was little, silly. I know it's hard to imagine with all this white hair and these big wrinkles, but I was a kid. Poppy was a kid. You see your dad over there?" Larry is still inspecting the tear in the screen. "He was even a kid." Nanny and Jason laugh in unison. "We are all actually a teeny bit jealous of you and your brothers."

"Really? Why is that?" Jason questions with confusion.

"Well, because these are some of the best times in your life. So enjoy them, treasure them, and never forget them. The last thing I wanted to ask is actually a favor. Listen, I know your dad is a lot to handle and is not always the most relaxed person. He loves you and your brothers very much! Will you promise Nanny you will always remember that?"

"Yes, Nanny. I will. I promise!" Jason responds as the two lovingly embrace.

It was clear after that conversation with my grandmother, the door that leads back to our childhood never really closes. There's no age limit of wanting to visit that special time and place. I could feel the emotion buried in her voice when she spoke to me about being a child.

I also remember the shock and absolute disbelief I felt when my grandmother reminded me that my father was once a kid! (chuckling) I mean really? How was this over-the-top, intense, high-strung man I called my father, once little like me? It was mind blowing, and it still is today. My grandmother knew my dad was wound tighter than a spool of fishing line. She also knew that underneath all of his crazy shenanigans, the admiration for his boys ran deep. It would be years before I would be able to fully comprehend the depth of his love.

The Magic of Mayfair

Chapter Ten
Trampoline Adventure

Summer of 1987

Four skateboards glide down the smoldering hot black-top. Each set of skateboard wheels hit the wooden launch ramp and soar high into the air. Jimmy, Jason, Bobby, and Donnie all land in a consecutive line and gracefully coast around the cul-de-sac. They quickly transition into performing an array of complex street tricks. The boys are seen playfully executing ollies, kick flips, and hand-plants.

"Yo! That method was so rad, Jay. You're getting really good! One day you're gonna be a better skater than me if you keep practicing!" shouts out Jimmy with laughter.

"One day? I think it's already happened," Jason declares. He slowly glides over toward Jimmy, leaps off his skateboard, and tackles him into the neighbor's front yard.

The two boys begin playfully tussling.

"Why don't you girls go get a room and stop fooling around on Ms. Mitchell's lawn!" Donnie blurts out from the street.

Ms. Mitchell pauses and waves at the boys with a smile as she weeds in her perfectly manicured flower garden.

With intense excitement, Bobby shouts out, "Hey, let's head over to the Thompsons! I heard they got a new HUMONGOUS trampoline in their backyard! We should go check it out! Mrs. Thompson told me we could use it whenever we wanted to!"

"Are you serious?!" Jason and Jimmy both question as they pause during their WWF wrestling match.

"LET'S GO!" yell all the boys in unison as they dash up the street toward the trampoline. The boys banter back and forth as they run.

"So, best looking goes first!" shouts out Jason.

"Then I guess it would be me," Donnie hollers back as he tries desperately to keep up with everyone.

Bobby responds, "You're so enormous you would go right through the tramp, Donnie!"

Jimmy kicks up the speed and easily pulls ahead of the group. He looks back and yells out laughing, "You're all a bunch of losers!"

The boys arrive at the Thompson's house and dart straight down the side yard in a single file line. Breathing heavily, they all get to the trampoline and immediately freeze in their tracks.

"WHOA!" Jason says to himself with genuine amazement.

Astonished, Donnie blurts out, "Look at the size of that thing!"

"Yeah, it's bigger than you, Don, and that's pretty damn big!" Bobby responds with his patented snort-laugh.

"Hi there, boys, how's everyone doing?" yells out Mrs. Thompson with excitement, waving from her patio.

Mrs. T. is casually watering her hanging plants, while standing on a step-stool. She's wearing her wide brim sun hat and oversized sunglasses.

"You're more than welcome to use the trampoline, just please be careful. No broken bones today," Mrs. Thompson requests with a sincere smile.

"OK! Thanks, Mrs. T!" the group shouts back with excitement.

Each boy takes his turn bouncing up and down as he skyrockets high into the air with exhilaration.

The clanking sound of the trampolines tightly wound metal springs can be heard from several houses away.

So, if you grew up any time before... Let's say 1990, just a friendly be careful was more than sufficient when you were doing something dangerous at a neighbor's house. There was no concern about lawsuits. In fact, if you did get hurt, you were more worried about your father calling you a moron for not being careful. (laughing) There were no court orders sent to your friend's parents. You see, it was a magical time to be a child. You lived outside in the warm summer air. You got into mischief. You built skateboard ramps. You went exploring in the woods. You played until the sun went down and the streetlights came on.

For some reason, we have since convinced ourselves that it's no longer OK to live that way. It is way too risky to let our kids go and explore the world by themselves. It was much safer "back then", things were "different".

Were they though? Have the very devices that we sleep with and can't seem to put down caused us to view life so differently than we did thirty years ago? Instant news, immediate feeds of negativity on our social media pages.

Has the world of play dates taken the place of our playgrounds? Have smart phones, taken away our children's smart ideas? Has playtime been replaced by screen time? I know one thing. I wouldn't have traded my childhood for anything in the world!

The boys take a break from jumping to have a quick huddle in the middle of the trampoline.

"Hey guys! Let's double-bounce Donnie!" yells out Jimmy with enthusiasm.

"No way! You're crazy! It's NOT happening!" replies Donnie as he tries to quickly scoot off the trampoline.

"That's a great idea! What, are you scared?" Bobby intimidates as he jokingly pulls Donnie's rattail.

"Um, scared? No! I'm not scared," Donnie confirms with a nervous laugh.

With excitement, Jimmy shouts out the master plan.

"OK, we're going to do this! Donnie, stand in the middle of the tramp and start jumping as high as you can. We will all wait on the edge. Then, right when you come down... All three of us will jump forward and land at the exact same time you do. We're gonna catapult you so freakin high into the air! I mean REALLY high! It's going to be rad! Trust me!

With immense hesitation Donnie responds, "I don't know about this one guys, it seems a little dangerous."

"Are you boys OK? Remember, only one person jumping at a time," Mrs. Thompson kindly reminds before she walks inside her house.

"All good, Mrs. T!" Bobby reassures with a thumbs up and a wink.

With a loud whisper, Bobby requests, "Come on! Let's go before anyone sees us!"

"Fine, but you better not bounce me too high. You know I'm way bigger than all of you. If I hit the ground it hurts A LOT more!" Donnie anxiously instructs.

"Dude, come on, stop worrying! We will take it easy on you," Jason chuckles.

With a serious tone, Jimmy directs, "OK, Don, start jumping! Jay and Bobby, you stand over here."

Jimmy places each boy in a corner and then walks to his side as Donnie begins cautiously jumping.

"Go higher, Don!" Bobby yells out.

"I'm jumping as high as I can!" Donnie shouts back with sweat dripping down his forehead.

The view from underneath the trampoline shows how much force Donnie is jumping with as the elastic netting is coming within inches of hitting the ground.

"OK, when I count to three, we ALL jump and land at the same exact time that Donnie does! Is everyone ready?" questions Jimmy with elation. One... Two...

OK, I'm going to hit the pause button here momentarily. If I'm being honest, this may have been one of the dumbest things we ever decided to do. OK, really it was the dumbest thing we decided to do. (chuckling) We totally disregarded Mrs. Thompson's one person jumping at a time rule. However, when your twelve years old sometimes things that seem hilarious in theory, turn out to be complete disasters in reality. I hate to say it, but up until now, this was actually freakin' hysterical! The look of pure terror on Donnie's face was absolutely priceless! I mean come on, this is classic. Unfortunately, what happens next was burned into my mind for the next thirty years. Once I hit the play button, things go downhill rather quickly. Are you ready?

And THREE!"

Appearing to be shot out of a circus cannon, Donnie is catapulted into the air five feet higher than everyone else. His arms and legs are flailing as he flies right over the gigantic trampoline. Landing feet first on the ground, a loud crack is heard as he viciously buckles to the ground. The three other boys bolt off the trampoline and dart to Donnie's aide.

In agony, with sweat streaming down his face, Donnie immediately cries out, "It's broken! It's broken!"

Jimmy grabs Donnie's hand and squeezes it firmly. He gently caresses Donnie's back to help soothe the intense pain.

With calm concern, Jimmy instructs, "Don, you're going to be OK. I promise. Jay! Run inside and tell Mrs. Thompson to call 911, QUICKLY! Donnie, look at me. Look at me in the eyes."

"IT HURTS!" Donnie wails out in pain.

"I know it does, but I need you to look at me. Try to breathe through your nose and out through your mouth."

Donnie attempts to follow the specific directions as Jimmy continues to coach him. Slowly, Donnie begins to calm down.

"Good job, you're doing great, Don. Just continue breathing and keep looking at me. I got you dude. I'm going to stay with you the whole time!"

Jason frantically sprints back outside with an update.

"Hey guys! Mrs. T. is calling an ambulance, RIGHT NOW!" Jason confirms as he takes a gulp of air.

"An ambulance!? Are you fucking kidding me?!" Donnie yells out with tears of terror in his eyes.

Petrified, Donnie quickly sits up as Jimmy attempts to gently push him back down to the ground.

Jimmy states with confidence, "Donnie, try and stay calm. Your ankle is probably broken, but you're going to be OK. The paramedics will bring you to the hospital and put a cast on it. You'll be back jumping on this trampoline in no time! I promise!"

With tears streaming down his face, Donnie looks at Jimmy, squeezes his hand and replies, "I must have looked like a giant meatball flying through the air!"

Chuckling, Jimmy responds, "I have to be honest, dude. Your face looked like you took a massive dump in your pants."

Donnie looks Jimmy in the eyes with gratitude, takes a deep breath, and finally smiles.

Minutes later, Mrs. T. shouts as she sprints outside, "The ambulance is here! Hang on, the paramedics are coming around the house now!"

Jimmy kneels down and graciously holds Donnie's hand as the EMT's jog into the back yard.

Donnie is carefully lifted onto the stretcher and wheeled out of the backyard as Jimmy continues to clench his hand the entire time.

That's why Jimmy was the leader of our crew. There was something incredibly special about him. There are certain times in life when you can see the soul of a person, the chemistry of their makeup. The day Donnie was flung into the air like a giant meatball was a day that I will always remember. Not because of the "freeze frame" of Donnie's face, or his cracked ankle, but because my best friend jumped in and showed so much love and compassion toward another person. There was no teacher or adult around watching. There was no "benefit" to running over and taking care of Donnie. Jimmy was just being a good human being. Those traits aren't taught, they are just who a person is. There is an old saying… Eventually, you become the type of person you hang around with the most. I was blessed to have Jimmy be that person.

Never, ever, underestimate the power of good and how that can be absorbed by another person. That day was extremely powerful for so many reasons. The most important lesson we all learned aside from talking our friend into doing something so stupid, was the observation of compassion… genuinely caring about another person. The older I get, the more I've realized that love and kindness are alive. There happening right now, this very second. Maybe, if we turned off the news and opened up our heart, we would start to see the truth. Good will always triumph over evil. That I know. It's up to us to find it, embrace it, and then live it. It is out there… I know it is.

The Magic of Mayfair

Chapter Eleven
The Future of Home Entertainment

Next morning

Jason and his three brothers are all quietly eating breakfast at the kitchen table.

"What's up, boys?! I bought something REALLY cool yesterday! I'll show you guys after you finish eating!" Larry blurts out with excitement from the family room.

"OK, Dad!" the boys shout back with anticipation.

Moments later, Larry darts into the kitchen wearing only white FRUIT OF THE LOOM underwear.

"So Toad, what the hell happened yesterday?! I heard Donnie broke his ankle on the Thompson's trampoline. I also heard all of you were jumping at the same time. I swear, you morons share one brain!" Larry yells out, shaking his head.

Hysterical, Eric begins to laugh uncontrollably.

"Shut up, Eric! Mind your own business!" Jason abruptly responds.

"Hey! Knock it off, Jason, or you're going to be punished. I promise I'll take away everything you own! Your skateboard, your NINTENDO, your bike, EVERYTHING! You'll be getting around on roller skates if you don't watch it. I mean it! I'm going in my room to get dressed. I don't want to hear any arguing or fighting. You got it?" Larry yells out with frustration.

Eric giggles again. Jason instantly clenches his fist and stares back at his brother with an angry scowl.

Larry returns a few minutes later, carrying a medium size, padded grey cloth bag.

With anticipation, Adam questions, "What's that, Daddy?"

All three older boys dash over as Larry swiftly places the bag on top of the kitchen counter.

Larry officially declares, "This gentleman… is the future of home movies!"

"What do you mean 'the future of home movies'? Dad, you sound like that weird sales guy who works at Radio Shack," Jason giggles with confusion.

Larry proudly unzips the mystery bag as he carefully reveals a state-of-the-art JVC home video camera.

"WHOA!" all the boys respond in awe.

"See this little tiny cassette, guys? This is the only thing that goes inside the camera. Once you're done, all you have to do is pop it out and put it into this VHS adaptor." Larry demonstrates, and then continues. "Then it just goes right into the VCR!" Larry brags with excitement.

"That's so awesome, Daddy! It's so small, like a little baby camera," Adam responds laughing.

With excitement, Jason blurts out, "Can you take some video of me skateboarding, Dad?"

"Sure, start behaving and I'll think about it." Larry responds as he jokingly flicks the side of Jason's head.

"Hey, who wants me to interview them?" Larry questions with elation.

"I do!" respond all three boys in unison with their hands stretched high in the air.

"OK, go in my office and I'll meet you there in a minute.

"Ellen, go get The Herm! I'm going to videotape the three stooges in my office."

"Come on, Larry, he's only two years old and you've already given Jared a ridiculous nickname!" Ellen reprimands.

The boy's dash into the office and all sit down at the arts and crafts table.

"You're in MY seat Eric, get up now, you bed-wetter!" Jason yells out as he tries to forcefully yank his brother out of the chair.

"Get off me! You don't own this seat!" Eric cries out.

"I said get up you idiot or I'll tell everyone you use that baby WEE-ALARM, because you PEE-PEE in your bed! Maybe you need to borrow one of Jared's diapers," Jason shouts out giggling.

"Hey, hey, knock it off, NOW!! What the hell are you animals fighting about? I swear you guys will never leave this house. Do you understand?" Larry exclaims with frustration.

Eric looks up with tears dripping down his cheeks and declares, "He's so mean to me! I didn't do anything!"

Frustrated, Larry lashes out, "Jason and Adam, go out and close the door... NOW! I want to talk to Eric, ALONE!"

"BUT, DAD," Jason whines.

"I SAID NOW, JASON!" Larry ferociously yells back as everyone in the room immediately becomes silent.

"Holy crap, I've never heard him scream that loud," Jason whispers to Adam as they quickly scamper out.

A fuzzy, grainy, 1980's-quality display screen is seen as Larry powers on the video camera and begins to record Eric.

"What's a matter, Berry? What happened? Why are you and Jason always fighting?" Larry calmly inquires.

"Daddy?" Eric softly questions with tears still in his eyes.

"Yeah, Buddy?" responds Larry.

"When I was born, did Jason hate me from the first time you brought me home from the hospital, or did it take some time? Did he ever want me to be his brother? Did he ever love me?"

After a short pause, Larry struggles to respond, "Eric... Ya know... Sometimes there are no answers for the reason why someone treats another person the way they do. I think your brother has some anger in him and unfortunately, he's decided to take it out on you. Jason's a good person and I really believe he has a good heart. Over time, I think he will understand how special you are and what a kind, caring person you have always been. Sometimes people need to find their own happiness, before they can start to be kind to others. I know it's not easy right now, but please try and ignore him. Hey, can I share a secret with you that I have never told anyone?"

With tenderness, Eric responds, "Sure, Daddy."

"Well, like I said, I have never told anyone this. It's not easy for me to admit. The way Jason treats you," Larry hesitates. "Well, I was kind of the same way to my younger brother. I wasn't very nice to him and didn't treat him with much kindness." Larry pauses and takes a deep breath. "He always wanted my attention and I couldn't stand being around him. He annoyed me and got on my nerves. I would call him very mean names and embarrass him in front of our friends. I wasn't nice to him at all. Then as I got older, I started to realize one of the main reasons I wasn't being a good big brother, was because I wasn't always happy. You see, it wasn't anything he did. Your Uncle

Michael just wanted my love. He just wanted me to include him in my life."

"Daddy... Are you crying? I think I see a tear falling down your face," Eric questions with sincere concern.

"I'm OK, buddy," Larry responds with a subtle laugh as he quickly wipes his eye (the camera shakes and then refocuses). Listen, I just wanted you to know, the way people treat you in life is not always because of anything you ever did to them. Some people just haven't found joy in their hearts and because they don't have it, they are mean to those people who love them most."

"Really?" questions Eric in wonder.

"I know, it doesn't make the most sense, but as you get older it will, pal. Just remember one thing and one thing always. You're a very special little boy. Your mom and I both love you very much. I know one day, Jason will see your kind spirit and warm heart. It may take him some time, but it will happen. I know it! You just keep being you and don't change." Larry takes another deep breath and slowly exhales. "Hey Berry, look at me. The next time Jason teases you about wetting your bed. You can remind him that he's afraid of the dark and has to sleep with the hall light on, at twelve years old!" They both laugh as Larry softly kisses Eric on his forehead.

"Thanks, Daddy. I love you." Eric responds as he smiles and hugs his father.

With reassurance, Larry replies, "Well, I love you most, Berry!"

Larry delicately turns the video camera off and the small display screen goes dark.

That video clip was powerful! You know, I didn't find that tape until years later when I was cleaning out our garage. I remember anxiously popping it into the VCR and was absolutely stunned by how vulnerable my father sounded. This was a man, who until I watched that video, I had never seen or heard any emotional side. In fact, if he really was crying during that interview, it was the only time I ever knew of that happening.

After watching this video, it all finally made sense to me. I was right all along. The reason it hurt my father so much when I mistreated my younger brother, was because he did the exact same thing to his. You see, regret is a difficult thing to live with and he knew it. My dad didn't want me making the same mistakes he did. I just wish he had the same conversation with me that he had with my brother Eric.

The beautiful thing about life is that cycles can be broken and people can change. After watching this video, it was clear to me how important it is as a parent to be honest with your children. Share your shortcomings and failures, just as often as you tell them about your successes. If the meaning of life is truly to leave this world a better place than when we found it, then we have to be honest. Not only to ourselves, but to the people we love. It's never too late to mend a wounded relationship, heal a broken heart, or help rescue someone you may have hurt. My dad taught me a valuable lesson that day, without me even being there to hear it.

Be kind and patient. Never forget that every person you walk by has their own story, their own pain, their own victories, and their own shame.

THE NEXT DAY

"Mom, I'm going to Jimmy's house!" Jason yells out with happiness as he bursts through the propped-opened front door.

Jason grabs his skateboard that is leaning against the wall on the front porch.

With his skateboard in one hand, Jason walks down the driveway in between both parked cars. He puts his board on the ground, hops on, and eagerly skates down the street toward Jimmy's house.

As Jason gets closer, he sees Jimmy in the distance. He hears the loud piercing sound of a power saw cutting through wood. Jason approaches Jimmy's house and stops his skateboard.

"Hey, dude! What are you cutting?" Jason yells out as he kicks his board into the grass and strolls up the driveway.

Jimmy doesn't answer as the roar of the circular saw is overpowering Jason's voice.

"JIMMY!" Jason yells out even louder.

Still with no response, Jason approaches Jimmy and gently taps his shoulder from behind.

Completely startled, Jimmy leaps up, drops the saw, and immediately grabs his finger. An intense grimace of pain can be seen on his face.

Blood slowly starts to trickle down Jimmy's wrist and forearm.

"Holy shit! I'm so sorry, dude! I didn't mean to scare you! I was just trying to get your attention!" Jason yells out with immense concern.

"It's OK, it's OK. Grab that towel over there by my dad's toolbox. It looks worse than it feels," Jimmy explains.

Darting over, Jason picks up a dirty, greasy, white dishrag off of the garage floor.

"Here, here, let me wrap it around your finger. We need to stop the bleeding. I'm so sorry, dude. I can't believe this happened." Jason apologizes as he presses the towel firmly around Jimmy's hand.

"It doesn't hurt anymore. I'm good, Jay, but it should be fun explaining to my parents why there's blood all over their driveway," Jimmy jokes with a nervous giggle.

"Let me find you a BAND-AID," Jason graciously offers.

After several minutes of observing Jason frantically scrambling through his garage, Jimmy removes the bloody towel. With shock, Jimmy shrieks, "OH MY GOD!" The tip of my finger is gone! IT's GONE! I cut it right off!"

Jason runs over hysterically crying as he embraces Jimmy while tears stream down his face.

With immense guilt, Jason closes his eyes and pleads, "I'm so sorry! It was an accident!" There's a short pause.

"Hey, Jay, chill out," Jimmy replies in a surprisingly calm voice.

Jason quickly looks up with a bewildered expression on his face.

"I'm just joking with you, dude. It's only this small cut by my nail. It's freaking amazing how bad it bled!"

"WAIT, WHAT? You didn't cut off the tip of your finger?" Jason confirms.

"Nope, it's good," Jimmy giggles.

"OK... I'M GONNA KILL YOU!" Jason yells out to the sky with massive relief.

Laughing, Jimmy responds, "I GOT YOU!"

"Damn, I was ready to run home to get my mom. UGH! I can't believe you were messing with me! Feel my heart, dude.

It's FREAKIN' pounding!" Jason confirms as he takes Jimmy's hand and places it on his chest.

"Shit, your heart is beating fast, Jay!" replies Jimmy with a smirk.

"Well, you're like a brother to me. So, of course when you scream out that I cut off your finger, I'm going to freak out you, A-Hole. I still can't believe you did that to me. Put this BAND-AID on. Oh, and what were you cutting anyway? Wood for a new launch ramp?" questions Jason.

"Naw, I need to replace parts of the tree house. Some of those 2x4's we climb up are rotting. I nailed those into the tree almost six years ago!" Jimmy advises.

"WOW, really?! Time sure flies," responds Jason with amazement. Jimmy teases, "Hey, since you cut off my finger, now you have to help me carry all these 2x4's over to the tree house."

Jason negotiates, "Well since you almost gave me a damn heart attack, you owe me lunch."

"Fine, I guess that sounds like a fair deal. My parents should be home by 12:00 o'clock, so I'll tell my mom to make us both lunch," Jimmy agrees.

Both boys scoop up the 2x4's, walk down the side of the house, and dump them like heavy bricks in front of the tree trunk.

The sun is glowing through the leaves of the peaceful tree as the cool morning summer breeze gently rattles the branches.

"Wow! She's getting really big!" Jason exclaims, as both boys look up at the tree.

In agreement, Jimmy responds, "I know! When we first moved in, only my little sister and I could fit up there. Now, she could hold both of our dads!"

Laughing, Jason responds, "Well, I'm not so sure about my dad!" There is a short pause. "Hey, have you ever noticed that the huge hole in her trunk looks just like a mouth? It's almost like she's smiling at us. I don't know what it is about this tree, Jim. Since the very first day I sat up there, it has always been so calming and relaxing. It just makes me feel... Well, happy. I can't really explain it."

"Yeah, I know exactly what you mean. Sometimes, at night, when I feel nervous, or sad... I sneak out of my house and just sit up there with my flashlight. It's so quiet and peaceful. You know, I actually fell asleep up there for a few hours one night," Jimmy reminisces.

"No way, really?" questions Jason with surprise.

"Yup, I swear, it felt like the tree wrapped her arms right around me. I felt safe. Like something was hugging me. Like nothing could go wrong," Jimmy attempts to explain.

Grateful, Jason responds, "Well, we're lucky she decided to grow in your yard."

"Yeah, it almost seems like she knew I was going to move here one day and was just waiting for me to come. Aww... I can't believe I'm actually talking about a tree, like it knows what we're saying," Jimmy chuckles as he shakes his head.

Jason pauses and slowly looks up at the tree.

He intently stares Jimmy in his eyes and responds with complete certainty, "She does."

Jimmy takes a deep breath and responds, "OK, well then, let's get those rotted boards off her! We need to put these new ones on, especially if we ever want to climb up there again. Jay, knock the first one off. Here's my hammer. You gotta smack it hard! Those boards have been nailed into that trunk for years!" Jimmy instructs with enthusiasm.

Jason responds with a chuckle, "OK, I'll think about when my brother Eric annoys me."

The boards start flying off the trunk as Jason begins to intensely smack them with the hammer.

"Jeez, dude, you must not like Eric. Those were some really hard hits. You know, I see you yelling at him sometimes. Eric seems like a good kid, Jay. You should try and go easy on him. He just wants to be your buddy. I actually wish I had a little brother, but I got stuck with two sisters that drive me crazy!" Jimmy explains with laughter.

"Yeah, well you can have him!" Jason responds as he begins to hammer the nails into the newly cut 2x4's.

Angrily, Jason begins to whack the nails harder and harder. Suddenly, he misses and smashes his finger with the hammer! With blood dripping down his wrist, Jason continues in extreme pain.

Concerned Jimmy shouts out, "Jay, Jay, STOP! What are you doing? Your finger is bleeding!" Not listening, Jason continues.

"STOP, NOW!" Jimmy screams out in frustration as he forcefully grabs Jason's arm in mid-swing. Stop, dude! What's wrong with you? It's like the minute you thought about your brother Eric, you went nuts. What the hell is going on?"

Jimmy quickly takes his t-shirt off and wraps it around Jason's bloody finger.

"Here, hold this on your hand. Let's take a break and go chill out in the tree house for a little bit. Be careful, some of the 2x4's are loose!" Jimmy yells back as he carefully climbs up.

Both boys make their way onto the platform. They slide over plastic milk crates and sit down on them. A cool breeze suddenly blows through their hair as a sense of calmness flows through Jason's body. The boys momentarily sit in pure silence. They direct their focus to the birds and squirrels bustling throughout the sturdy tree branches.

"Sorry, Jim. I don't know what got me so upset down there. I'm not sure why I get so mad and angry sometimes," Jason wonders with regret.

"It's OK, dude. I understand. Trust me, I do. How's your finger?" questions Jimmy.

"Sore, but I think it will be OK," Jason responds as he carefully unwraps the shirt from his hand.

Jimmy cringes from the bloodstains.

"Oh, here's your t-shirt," Jason reminds as he attempts to toss it back.

With disgust, Jimmy replies, "You mean YOUR shirt, now! Yeah, I'm not touching that again!" Both boys start to laugh.

"Thank you," Jason simply replies with sincere gratitude.

With confusion Jimmy questions, "For what?"

"Well, for being like a big brother to me. Ya know, I guess I just get tired of being the oldest sometimes. For some reason, I take it out on Eric. You're right dude, he is a good kid." Jason takes a deep breath. "I've never have told anyone this before, but sometimes I feel bad for the way I treat him. I know it really upsets my dad when he sees me yell at him. That makes me sad," Jason confesses as tears begin to well up in his eyes.

With understanding, Jimmy responds, "I know how you feel. Everyone has anger and sadness inside them sometimes. Just do your best to try and control it. I know it isn't easy. Jay... You know anytime you want to come up here, you can. This is our tree. It always will be. One day when we have our own kids, we will still come up here and look up at the stars. We will always remember the amazing times we had together." There is a short pause. "Jay... blood brothers?" Jimmy questions as he carefully takes off his BAND-AID.

Jason proudly responds as he looks down at his bloody finger, "Blood brothers!"

With emotion, the boys interlock their hands for several seconds and then smile with pride.

That was the day I realized that there's people you meet in life that you feel connected to by the other person's soul. You just "get them" and they "get you". It's effortless. I had only known Jimmy for about five years at that point, but it felt like we were destined to be life brothers. That day we were. We had a bond that would be with us forever, regardless of distance or circumstance. It was unbreakable. I would be there for him and I just knew he would always be there for me. (pausing) And, what about our tree? Well... They're some things in life that you can't really explain. It "just is". There was magic on that street... That I know. For me, it all connected back to that oak tree. It was our home base, where we spent countless hours talking, laughing and arguing. Through it all, we always felt as those roots continued to grow, so would our friendship. As long as our tree was still standing, so were all of our magical memories.

Chapter Twelve
The Roller Coaster We Call Life

Late Summer 1989

Jason is crammed into the backseat of Jimmy's 1985 Mustang as he is being driven down Mayfair Court. Mr. Gallo is sitting in the passenger seat. Jimmy's hands firmly clench the steering wheel, with the look of intense concentration and nervousness.

"Not bad son, not bad! You were riding that old ladies ass on Landmark and scared the shit out of me when you stopped short on 580, but overall you did good. A couple of more lessons and I think you may be ready to take your driving test in a few months. Jay, whatcha think? How did Jimmy do?" Mr. Gallo questions with his deep intimidating voice.

"Um, pretty good! Although I have to admit, I squeezed the door handle so hard I may have ripped it off," Jason jokes with laughter.

Mr. Gallo directs, "Son, pull in behind Mom's car."

Jimmy follows his father's orders as he cautiously pulls into his driveway.

Relieved, Jimmy finally puts his Mustang in park as beads of sweat trickle down the sides of his temples.

"Dinner in an hour!" Mr. Gallo shouts as he gets out and slams the car door closed.

"You OK, dude? Ya look like you just ran a marathon. You're covered in sweat," Jason laughs.

"Shit, Jay, you know how my dad is! I was fucking crapping my pants the entire time!" Jimmy explains with a deep breath.

"Well, let me out, I'm also sweating my ass off back here!" Jason pleads.

Jimmy exits the car and manually moves the seat forward so Jason can squeeze out of the back seat.

"Are you allowed to hang for a little bit?" questions Jason as he stretches his legs.

Reaching into his pocket, Jimmy responds, "Yeah, I have some time!"

The boys walk in front of the car and sit on the hood. Jimmy pulls out a cigarette and a plastic lighter.

With surprise and concern, Jason asks, "Where the hell did you get that from?"

"I grabbed a couple out of my dad's pack. He'll kick my ass if he finds out. Oh, and don't do what I'm doing! This shit is bad for you!" Jimmy responds as he cups his hand and lights up his cigarette. Both boys laugh.

"Then why are you doing it, dude?" questions Jason as he chuckles.

"Well, because it relaxes and calms me down," replies Jimmy as he blows a cloud of smoke high into the air.

With excitement, Jason blurts out, "I can't believe you're going to get your license in September! It's so freaking awesome! That was really nice of your parents to buy you a car."

"Yeah it was, but I have to work my ass off to pay them back. I don't feel like wasting my summer bagging groceries when I could be hanging out with my friends. Jay, I promise I'll be driving you everywhere. Think about it. Anywhere we want to go! We just jump in my car and do it! Skate parks, Clearwater Beach, road trips to Miami. It's gonna be so rad!" Jimmy declares as he takes another puff from his cigarette.

"Yeah man, I can't wait! It's like the next chapter of our life is getting ready to start," Jason responds.

"Yup and don't worry, I'll make sure I introduce you to everyone I know in school this year. High school is pretty awesome. Plus, there's *a ton* of hot girls that go there. They will love you, Jay. Those big green eyes are so irresistible," jokes Jimmy with a feminine voice.

"You're funny, dude," Jason replies as he shakes his head.

Both boys casually lean back on the car and put their arms behind their head as they look up at the clouds in the sky.

In deep thought, Jimmy shares, "Man, it's hard to believe how fast we are growing up. Before we know it, we will be in college, then married. You know, sometimes I wonder what my future wife is doing at the exact second I'm thinking about her. She could be living right down the street for all I know, or in another state."

"Or, she could be making out with another, guy," Jason jokes as both boys laugh.

"Yeah, for some reason that's the stuff I think about. Oh, shit! I gotta head in. My dad's gonna start screaming if I'm not ready. We're going over to my pop's house for dinner tonight," Jimmy shouts out as he hops off the hood of the car.

He runs down the driveway and flicks the cigarette bud into the sewer.

"How's your grandfather doing?" asks Jason with concern.

Jimmy responds with a deep breath, "He is doing pretty well for his age. He's getting old, but he still has his sense of humor and his "New Joy-sey" accent." Both boys begin to chuckle.

"Hey, call me tomorrow!" Jimmy yells out as he runs inside and slams the front door closed.

JOY AND HAPPINESS

Leaving Jimmy's driveway, Jason begins to stroll down the wide concrete sidewalk toward his house. The sun is setting as warm glowing shades of red, yellow, and orange wrap around the sky. Jason cheerfully waves at a neighbor getting into their car as young children happily ride their bicycles past him. A few houses down, Ms. Mitchell is watering her front lawn. Jason momentarily stops and chats with her. They smile and then embrace with a hug. Continuing to walk, Jason approaches the sewer in front of his house and sits down on it. He takes a deep breath, looks up at the tranquil sunset and smiles with jubilation. A car passes by with young children as they press their faces against the passenger side window. Jason waves at them and laughs. Life on Mayfair Court is absolutely marvelous!

THE NEXT MORNING

Jason wakes up earlier than normal and begins to get dressed for the day. Surprisingly, he overhears an intense conversation brewing from inside his parent's room. Cautiously, Jason creeps up to the slightly opened door and begins to intently listen.

LARRY'S VOICE

"I'm telling you, Ellen, it's the right thing to do! They're getting older! It's gonna get much more difficult for them to make the long drive to see us. Our kids are young, now's the time to make the move!

"There's *tons* of construction happening in Coral Springs. The entire neighborhood is brand new. We can actually design and build our own home!

"The schools are all top-rated and not far at all from where our parents live. Ten to fifteen minutes, tops! Lots of younger families are moving into that part of the city.

"I'll be able to work from home on the days I'm not traveling. And the best part, your mother will be there to help out when I'm out of town! Trust me, if we don't do it now, we will miss our chance!"

Jason steps closer to the door and tries to concentrate on what exactly is being discussed.

ELLEN'S VOICE

"I don't know, Larry. I just don't know! You're REALLY pushing this on me and I DO NOT like it! Where did this come from?

They love it here! They're happy! I'm happy! We've made this our home.

"And what about Jason, he's going to be starting high school in the fall. He's fourteen-years-old... FOURTEEN-YEARS-OLD! It's hard enough to make that transition in the same neighborhood, with the same friends, let alone not knowing a single person. I'm not letting you push this one on me, Larry. Not this time! It doesn't feel like the right thing to do, for me, or for the kids. Especially for Jason! I see the happiness in his eyes everyday, growing up on this street.

"It's the same joy you had growing up on Adelle Road. Think of all the incredible memories you treasure and hold close to your heart. You're always talking about how lucky you were to grow up in such an amazing neighborhood. Why would you want to rip that same blessing away from your son?" Ellen takes a deep breath.

"No Larry, I'm not doing it! I have to do what's best for my children, not what's best for us!"

With a stunned look, Jason turns around. He slowly tippy-toes out of the house and softly closes the front door.

I could hardly comprehend what had just transpired. The shock pulsated through my entire body and joy flowed through my veins. This was an epic day! The unimaginable had just occurred. My mother *finally* stood up to my father's smothering sales pitch! I remember vividly celebrating her victory as I fist pumped high in the air. I wanted to burst through their bedroom door and high five her!

They say that mothers know their children better than anyone, and she knew my heart was connected that street. She understood that certain things in life are truly blessings and living on Mayfair Court was one of them.

ONE WEEK LATER

Bobby, Jimmy, and Jason are all skateboarding back from the nearby mall. They slowly start to head down their street and recap the action-packed day. Jason quickly looks up and glances at the Mayfair Court street sign and smiles.

"Bobby! I can't believe your sister actually hooked us up with lunch, dude! I think she gave us every type of hot dog they sell!" Jason shouts out in shock.

"Stop talking about hot dogs. I'm seriously about to puke," Jimmy warns.

"Cheese dog, chili dog, bacon dog," Jason teases.

"Dude, I'm telling you, please stop or you're gonna be sorry," Jimmy pleads, holding his stomach.

Bobby jokes, "Well, I made the mistake of esca-sliding right after eating. I burped up hot dogs everywhere!"

"You're so nasty man! And what the hell is esca-sliding?" Jason questions.

"While you were flirting with Amy at the music store, Jimmy and I went to go do it! It's when you slide down the middle section of the two escalators. It's so much freaking fun! How do you not know what that is, dude? The security guard who looks like John Candy ran over and almost kicked us out of the mall," responds Bobby, with his obnoxious snort-laugh.

"Damn! That sounds so rad! I gotta try that next time we go. Except I won't eat the FRENCH FRY DOG!" Jason shouts out deliberately, so Jimmy hears him.

"Shut up, Jay!" Jimmy yells back, laughing.

"Hey, Jay, my parents are gone this weekend. We're going to chill at my house later if you want to come over. I'm gonna set up my mom's exercise trampoline and have a back-flipping competition into the pool!" Bobby announces with excitement.

Laughing, Jason responds, "Just don't invite Donnie over or you'll have no water left in the pool." The boy's all chuckle. "Thanks man, but I gotta get going. It's Eric's birthday today. I told my parents I'd actually come home for cake."

"OK, well if you finish early, just walk inside. We will be in the pool," Bobby responds.

"Yeah, sounds good. I'll see you guys later." With a loud pretend cough, Jason blurts out, "CORN DOG!" then starts laughing as he quickly skates away!

The boys stop and wave goodbye to Jason as they skate up Bobby's driveway.

"Going home for his brother's birthday to have cake? What the hell is that about? I thought he can't stand Eric?" Bobby questions Jimmy with confusion.

"Ya got me," Jimmy replies with a shoulder shrug.

Jason continues to skateboard down the street toward his house as he gracefully glides from side-to-side. Surprised, in the distance he notices something odd in his front yard. From afar he's not sure exactly what it is. As Jason gets closer, he can see there's a long wooden object of some sort. It's sticking into the ground with something hanging from it. Panicked, Jason pops up his skateboard, secures it under his arm, and begins to run. With each house he passes, the vision becomes more and more vivid. Breathing heavily, Jason sprints as fast as possible, until he arrives at his front yard. He freezes and frantically stares for several seconds.

Suddenly, with his heart beating through his chest, Jason takes his skateboard and slams the FOR-SALE sign as hard as he possibly can! He throws his skateboard to the ground and dashes up the driveway. He rips open the front door and bolts inside. The family is in the middle of singing happy birthday to Eric.

Sweaty and out of breath, Jason screams out crying, "What the hell is in our yard, Dad?! Mom, I heard you telling Daddy we weren't moving! You said you wouldn't do that to me. You lied! You fucking lied! I hate you both for doing this to me! I'M NOT MOVING!"

Eric innocently asks his dad if he can open his presents. "SHUT YOUR DAMN MOUTH, ERIC!" Jason ferociously screams out with resentment.

"HEY!!! SHUT YOUR DISGUSTING MOUTH, JASON!" Larry snaps back with anger pulsating through his voice.

With despair, Ellen responds. "I'm so sorry, Jason. The realtor wasn't supposed to put the sign up until tomorrow. We came home and it was already there. We were planning on talking to you about this tonight. I would never have wanted you to find out this way. Please, believe me!"

Devastated, Jason breaks down and begins to hyperventilate. He collapses to the ground and struggles to cry out, "WHY?! WHY?! WHY?!"

Ellen glares at Larry with resentment and shakes her head in frustration.

She walks over, kneels on the ground, and begins to comfort Jason by softly rubbing his back.

Attempting to console her heartbroken son, Ellen emotionally replies, "It's going to be OK. I promise. Listen, we will be so close to your grandparent's. Daddy's right, Jason. I really do need their help during the week."

"Listen, we're looking at buying a brand-new house, in a really nice neighborhood. Just like this one, maybe even nicer!" Jason continues to cry out loud. "There's tons of kids there you'll meet. Daddy said there's even a skateboard park, not far from the house. Your friends can come and visit us. You can come back here on vacations. We will make it work. I promise."

With bloodshot eyes, Jason slowly stands up, hugs his mother, and places his head on her shoulder.

Struggling to stop crying, Jason responds as he tries to catch his breath, "Mom, I'm going to miss it here, so, so, so, much. I'm going to miss everything about it. My friends, all my memories, this house, it's going to be so hard."

Ellen lovingly caresses Jason's head and reassures, "I know, honey... I know. Everything is going to be OK."

A tear trickles down her face.

LATER THAT EVENING

Larry is comfortably reclined in his lazy boy sofa chair with Jared sitting on his lap. He is watching PET SEMATARY on television in the family room. Eric and Adam are sitting on each arm of the chair.

"Where are you going?!" Larry questions with emotion as Jason darts past him.

Still devastated, Jason shouts back, "OUT!" as he slams the front door closed.

Jason walks down his driveway and sits on the sewer in front of his house. The sun has set and the night sky is filled with bright sparkling stars.

Closing his eyes, Jason takes a deep breath, and then looks up at the moon's silhouette. The street is silent. The night breeze strengthens as the wind blows through his hair.

After taking a few minutes to calm himself down, Jason stands up and wipes away the tears from his eyes.

The illuminated streetlights capture Jason's shadow as he begins to trudge down the street. Moments later, he approaches Jimmy's side yard and walks directly toward the tree house. Jason pauses, and then starts to cautiously climb up each 2x4. He diligently tries not to make any noise.

Without warning, the last 2x4 cracks and falls to the ground.

"Shit!" Jason whispers to himself.

He gets onto the first level platform and fumbles to find Jimmy's flashlight. Lying down on his back, Jason closes his eyes. The night breeze continues to strengthen. The leaves and branches flurry in the wind. Suddenly, the air becomes calm and there is pure silence.

Noticing the bloodstained shirt that is still there, Jason balls it up into a pillow. He rolls over onto his side, takes a deep breath, and begins to quickly drift off. Falling into a semi-conscious state, Jason begins to have several intense emotional flashbacks:

Blissfully swimming under water in tranquil silence, while his house is still under construction.

The roar of the moving truck engine, as it slowly drives down Mayfair Court. The day Jason moved in.

Meeting Jimmy for the first time behind the moving truck. The feeling of excitement and nervousness is replicated as emotion steadily flows through Jason's body.

Sitting on the tree house platform, slowly interlocking hands as Jason and Jimmy become blood brothers.

There is a dark gloomy grey sky. It's filled with ferocious thunder, howling winds, and torrential rain. Jason is soaking wet as he viciously stares directly at the FOR-SALE sign. Suddenly, he unleashes a scream so loud it rattles the hanging metal sign. "NOOOOOO!" Gasping for air, Jason turns around and frantically attempts to run away as fast as he can.

"HEY!" startled, Jason's eyes flash wide open as Jimmy is staring directly at him from a few inches away.

Breathing heavily, Jason responds, "Jeez dude, you scared the hell out of me!"

"Well, I saw a light on up here and had a feeling it was you. What's going on? You look like shit, dude. Why are your eyes blood shot?" Jimmy questions with deep concern.

With fresh tears trickling down his face, Jason pauses and responds with emotion, "Well, last week I overheard my parents talking about moving away so we could live closer to my grandparents in Coral Springs. My mom basically told my dad it wasn't happening and she wouldn't do that to me! So, I thought the conversation was over. I figured it was just my annoying fucking dad, trying to talk my mom into something else, AGAIN! You know, the next best thing, like he always does." Jason pounds his fist on the tree house platform. "I'm actually shocked we've lived on this street as long as we have. The guy is never content and now he's ruining my entire life!"

In awe, Jimmy questions, "So they ended up telling you tonight?"

Frustrated, Jason grits his teeth and blurts out with a whisper, "OF COURSE NOT, MAN! After we got home from the mall earlier today, I saw the damn FOR-SALE sign in my front yard! A big ass, FOR SALE sign! At first I thought it was a mistake and someone put it at the wrong house."

In total disbelief, Jimmy puts both hands on his head, "Jesus Christ, dude, I can't believe what you're telling me! This doesn't even seem real."

"What the hell am I going to do, Jim? I'm really scared as shit man. I'm afraid of leaving here. I'm beyond petrified of starting high school in a place where I don't know a fucking soul!" Jason confesses with resentment.

With a comforting tone and deep breath, Jimmy responds, "It's going to be OK, dude. We will write each other letters all the time. I'll be visiting. You know I already have my car and once I get my license, I'll be driving down to see you all the time. It's only a four hour drive to Coral Springs." Jimmy takes a deep breath. "Listen, our friendship isn't going to change, I promise. Hell, I'll even bring Bobby with me to annoy the shit out of you. Like I said, it will be OK, I promise!" Each boy puts their arm around the other's shoulder.

Jason and Jimmy's shadowy silhouettes can be seen in the tree house as they talk late into the night. The only brightness is coming from the small flashlight.

I know now, the day my dad made the decision to leave Mayfair Court he did have the best intentions for his family. However, it was true. He was always searching for the next best car, the next best house, in the next best town. It's just who he was. As I got older, I learned to accept my dad and the choices he made. He was the best father he could be and in the end that's all I could ask for.

It was time to say goodbye and finish up this chapter of my life. Sure, I was devastated that I was going to leave the one place that brought me so much comfort and happiness. However, I knew in my heart that no distance would ever diminish my love for Mayfair Court and every single person who lived on that street.

I have one question for you... Do you believe in Magic? I do...

Chapter Thirteen
The Agony of Goodbye

Two months later

The moving truck pulls up in front of the Shapiro house.

The driver knocks on the door and politely requests, "Hey, Mr. Shapiro, would you mind moving your car out of the driveway so we can pull up closer to the house?"

"Wait, you want me to park my brand-new Cadillac in the street?" There is a short pause. "I'll be out in a few minutes!" Larry responds, throwing his arms up in frustration.

At the same time, Jason walks out of his garage wearing his childhood HE-MAN backpack. It's filled with snacks for the road trip.

Looking up at the sky, Jason smiles as the sunlight warms his face. He glances over at the moving truck and notices two long legs on the opposite side. Chuckling, Jason shakes his head, and briskly walks down the driveway. He proceeds to jog around the moving truck. Jason and Jimmy immediately make eye contact and begin laughing.

They slowly walk up to each other and embrace with emotion. "Well, it looks like we're going to end this story the same way we started it," Jason jokes with a smile.

"Nice backpack," Jimmy teases with laughter.

"Umm, yeah, it's my little brother's," Jason responds as he snickers.

"My parents went to drop my sister off at her dorm, but they told me to tell you good luck and they will miss you," Jimmy informs.

Jason questions with a chuckle, "Your dad actually misses people?"

"Good one. Listen, you better call me as soon as you get to your new house and send me some pictures of the beaches down there. I hear there even nicer than the ones we have," requests Jimmy.

"You know I will," Jason replies, as he puts his hands on both of Jimmy's shoulders and looks him in the eyes.

"Listen Jay, I wrote you a letter," Jimmy shares.

"Wait, you wrote me a letter?" Jason questions with laughter.

"Yeah, I wrote a letter, dude. I was going to give it to you before you left today, but I decided to leave it in the tree-mouth. It will be waiting for you. So, you better come back to visit very soon, 'cause it took me forever to write it!" Both boys laugh.

With absolute certainty, Jason confirms, "I'll be back. I don't know when, but I will be and I promise I will read it."

"TOAD! It's time to go, pal!" Larry yells as he slowly walks out of his house for the last time.

Startled, Jason yells back, "OK Dad! I'll be there in a minute!"

Ellen shouts out with a warm smile, "Bye, Jimmy. You take care of yourself!"

Jimmy responds, fighting back tears, "Goodbye, Mrs. Shapiro, bye, Mr. Shapiro."

All the Shapiro brothers run down the driveway and lovingly hug Jimmy, one at a time. Then they each skip back to their car.

The moving truck air brake pops, signaling to the neighbors that this is the time for everyone's final goodbyes.

Slowly, the surrounding neighbors begin to walk out of their front doors. They all rush over toward Jason, Larry, and Ellen. They embrace them all with emotional good-bye hugs.

Jimmy turns to Jason.

"OK, Jay, I'm going to head home. I gotta make sure my little sis isn't trashing the house with her crazy friends. My parents put me in charge!" Jimmy flaunts proudly.

Sarcastically, Jason teases, "You're in charge? Jeez, that's really scary, dude."

Both boys start laughing and then powerfully embrace for the very last time.

Jimmy begins to walk back toward his house. Standing motionless, Jason watches as his life-friend walks away. Turning around before entering his driveway, Jimmy waves a final good-bye.

Jason continues to watch, until Jimmy is no longer in site. Heartbroken, Jason walks over to his father's car. The Shapiro's open the car doors and proceed to enter. Gradually, Larry backs out of the driveway, gives four farewell honks, and slowly drives up the street.

As the car drives away:

And as clearly as I remember this amazing journey beginning, it was time for it to end. Sometimes in life, there are just no answers to why things happen or why circumstances change. One thing I know is that the most powerful gift we are born with is the gift of memory. The ability to snap a picture so clear, we remember every detail as if it just happened. How beautiful it is to close our eyes and visit that memory whenever we want to. It's like turning on the television to your favorite channel. We can absolutely relive any moment and recapture time. That's pretty darn special. Sometimes turning on certain channels comes with hurt and pain... But if you can push through it, the ones we love will never be forgotten.

As it turned out, I never did end up going back to Mayfair Court. However, there were many nights I was able to visit in my dreams.

Beginning my next journey was an emotional struggle. Our new house felt empty and our street was lifeless. Vacant lots and partially built homes lined the neighborhood roads. The sound of echoing laughter was replaced by the roaring engines of cement trucks and bulldozers. It would be a long time before there was any resemblance of the place I grew up and called my home.

As the years went on, the void in my heart still remained. The memories of my childhood would often be triggered by subtle reminders of the past.

Incredible as it was living on Mayfair Court for those seven wonderful years... Like most people, my life was on course to take some very unexpected and painful turns. And even though years would separate each heartbreaking instance, it still felt like a barrage of uppercuts to my soul.

Chapter Fourteen
Up Against the Ropes

July 1998

Jason is feverishly typing on his computer as he sits at the kitchen table in his apartment. The room is dim. The only light is coming from a small lamp in the corner. Suddenly, the cordless house phone rings.

"Hello?" Jason calmly answers.

Distraught, Larry provides an unexpected update, "Hey, it's your dad. I wanted to let you know the police found your brother outside on campus in the snow again early this morning. This time, he was barely coherent and is being treated for hypothermia. They think he was out there for hours." Larry pauses and takes a deep breath. "You know he's been really struggling over the last few months. They took him to a local state mental hospital. The doctors have been evaluating him all day and confirmed," Larry pauses again. "That he is suffering from severe mental illness, Jason."

"Wait, what? I'm confused. What are you talking about, Dad?" Jason questions with concern.

Emotionally exhausted, Larry responds, "It is not good news. From the early diagnosis, the doctor thinks he has been living with paranoid schizophrenia for the last year, or maybe even longer. It's very difficult to tell for sure. This is a horrific disease. He was probably born with it and was just a matter of time until all the symptoms showed up. From what I've been told, it sounds like this disease typically hits adult men in their twenties."

"So, what's going to happen to him now?" Jason questions overcome with emotion.

Larry struggles to respond, "They are going to keep him hospitalized for now until they can get him stable, but it's not looking good. He's in bad shape. The doctor told me he's also been hearing voices. Listen, Jason, I gotta go. I fly out first thing in the morning. I'll call you when I get to the hospital and have more details. OK?"

Fighting back tears, Jason struggles to respond, "OK, Dad. Please, send him my love."

Jason hangs up the phone and collapses to the ground as he begins to have an emotional breakdown.

"NOOO! WHY?!" Jason screams out as he repeatedly pounds the desk with his fist.

"ERIC!!!" Jason cries out as all the years of guilt for the way he mistreated his little brother boil to the surface.

Beautiful flashbacks of innocent images from Eric's childhood rush through Jason's mind.

"I'm so sorry! GOD, I'm so sorry!" Jason repeats over and over and over…

April 2006

Excitement fills the air. Jason's fiancée Andrea is driving her car as Jason anxiously squirms in the passenger seat. They're visiting his hometown of Clearwater, Florida.

"WOW! I can't believe I finally made it back home. Unbelievable! I'm so excited for you to meet him! It's been so many years since we have seen each other." Jason blurts out with intense enthusiasm.

Andrea questions, "I'm so happy for you, babe. So, when was the last time you saw each other?"

Quickly, Jason responds, "Well, the day I moved off the street. Almost... Umm... Let's see..." Jason counts on his fingers. "Seventeen years ago. My GOD, has it been that long?! I mean, over the years we stayed in touch with letters and phone calls. We would even chat on AOL Instant Messenger, but it's actually been a while since I heard from him. You know, it's weird, he just kind of disappeared. I'm not even sure where he's living now. Last I remember, he moved back in with his parents and was working as a mechanic. I know he loved cars. He sent me so many pictures over the years of all the different Mustangs he had. I wonder what he's driving now. You know what, before we drive all the way out to my old street, let me call his parents just to make sure he's still living there." Jason pauses. "You know, I still remember their phone number."

"WOW! Are you serious? Jeez, I can't even remember the phone number I have now," Andrea responds with laughter.

"Yeah, I know, it's crazy. I must have called that phone number a *million* times," Jason reminisces with a smile.

"OK, I'm going to call now. Hopefully he answers, that would be amazing! Wish me luck," Jason requests as he takes a deep breath.

He dials the phone number on his cell phone and looks at Andrea with a big smile filled with nervous energy.

"It's ringing!" Jason replies as he fist pumps in the air. Andrea smiles and gives Jason a thumbs-up. The phone rings several times.

"Shit! No one's answering," Jason updates disappointedly.

There is a short pause. "Mr. Gallo?" Jason excitedly questions.

"Hey! It's me, Jason Shapiro. I'm in town with my fiancé and I was wondering if you knew where Jimmy was? I was hoping to see him while I was up here. Last time we spoke he mentioned he was living with you." A few seconds pass.

Jason's face begins to go pale as the expression of devastation comes over him.

"What?" Jason questions as he gasps for air.

"Are you OK?" Andrea whispers.

Slowly shaking his head side to side, Jason mouths, "NO!"

"Oh my GOD, Mr. Gallo, I'm so sorry." There is another short pause. "I'm so sorry. I had no idea." A few more seconds pass. "I love you all, too. OK... Bye."

Stunned, with tears in his eyes, Jason abruptly requests, "Can you please pull over? NOW!"

"Sure, baby. What's the matter? Tell me!" Andrea pleads.

Jason stares directly into her eyes.

With shock and disbelief, Jason replies, "He's gone. He's gone."

"What happened? Tell me!" Andrea begs.

Stunned, Jason attempts to explain, "He took his life last year. His dad said he was battling severe depression for years. I had no idea, absolutely no idea."

Jason hunches over in the car seat and put's both hands on his forehead. He begins to uncontrollably cry as he squeezes Andrea's hand. She tenderly rubs Jason's back and tries her best to console him. The sound of pain, devastation, and raw emotion is heard from inside the car.

MARCH 2013

Jason is at work sitting down in his office. He is taking a conference call on speaker phone.

"Great job, everyone! I am so proud of your performance this quarter. Your teams have really worked hard over the last several weeks. We're really starting to build some momentum!" Jason's boss exclaims.

Suddenly, Jason notices that his cell phone is continuously ringing on vibrate mode. He checks and sees four missed calls that display, MOM CELL on the screen. As soon as his conference call ends, he quickly hangs up and calls his mother back. The phone begins to ring.

Frantic, Ellen immediately answers, "Jason, your father was in a car accident! I'm not sure how bad it is, but the police are at our house. They want to talk to you. Hang on."

There is a short pause while Ellen passes off her phone. "Good afternoon, Jason. This is Detective D'Ambrosio with the Coral Springs Police Department." The detective pauses.

"Unfortunately, your father was involved in a car accident at approximately 2:35 pm this afternoon near his home. We aren't sure of his condition at this time. Are you able to leave work and take your mom over to the hospital?"

"Yeah, yeah, of course, I'm leaving now," Jason replies with extreme concern.

"OK, I'll let your mother know that you're on your way," the detective replies in a calm tone.

Jason darts over to the other manager working on the sales floor and informs with emotion, "I have to go! I just found out my father was in a car accident."

With understanding, the manager replies, "Sure, go! Is he OK?"

"I think so. He only drives short distances, locally. I'm sure it's just a fender-bender. I'll probably be back in a couple of hours," Jason responds with confidence as he jogs out to his car.

He gets in and begins to drive over to his parent's house. Moments later, Jason arrives and aggressively pulls into his mother's driveway.

Hysterical, Ellen steps into the car and frantically yanks the door closed. They speed away and pull into the hospital parking lot thirty minutes later.

Jason and Ellen get out of the car and scamper through the emergency room front doors. They see Jason's brother, Adam walking toward them shaking his head with tears in his eyes.

"Mom, stay here for a minute. Let me talk to Adam and see what's going on. I'm sure dad is fine," Jason directs with a soothing tone.

Jason approaches Adam and the two brothers embrace.

Heartbroken and struggling to speak, Adam provides an update, "He's not doing well. Dad's on a ventilator, man. They don't know if he's going to make it."

"What the hell are you talking about, dude?! How can that be? Mom said the accident happened right down the street from their house. I figured he had a few bumps and bruises," Jason responds in complete shock.

"It was a really bad accident, Jason! He was t-boned by a huge pickup truck and dad wasn't wearing his seat belt." Adam pauses. "Promise me you won't repeat what I'm about to tell you to mom. I don't want to upset her anymore than she already is."

Confused, Jason responds, "I won't, Adam. Tell me, what the hell happened?"

144

Heartbroken, Adam explains, "The detective told me he thinks dad got distracted when he answered his cellphone. The phone records show mom called him around the exact time of the accident." Adam pauses again and takes a deep breath. "The detective believes that dad took off his seatbelt while he was driving to take his cellphone out of his pocket."

"Oh my GOD!" Jason replies as he struggles to comprehend what has happened.

"Adam Shapiro."

"Yes! That's me," Adam promptly responds.

"Adam, I'm the lead trauma surgeon evaluating your father right now. Can you all step into my office?"

With tears in his eyes, Adam directs, "Yes, of course. Mom, the surgeon is calling us in. He needs to speak to everyone." Jason's youngest brother Jared has now also arrived. Everyone promptly follows the surgeon into his office.

"Please, sit down. I'm very sorry to have to be the bearer of this news. I really am. Your father suffered severe traumatic head injuries as a result of the car accident he was in earlier today. As you know, he is currently not breathing on his own. We have done multiple scans and all the tests are coming back with no evidence of any brain stem reflexes."

"WHAT DOES THAT MEAN?!?!" Ellen lashes out at the doctor with tears streaming down her face.

"Mrs. Shapiro... Your husband is brain dead. We can continue to stabilize his breathing by ventilating him, but I'm afraid there is nothing else we can do. His brain is no longer telling his body to breathe. Once his breathing stops, so will his heart." Ellen collapses to the ground as all the boys scramble to try and comfort her. "I would suggest you all take a few minutes together and strongly consider signing a DNR," the doctor explains.

"WHAT'S THAT?! Speak so I can understand you!!" Ellen shrieks out in hysterics.

"I'm sorry, Mrs. Shapiro, I apologize. That's an agreement you would sign stating that if your husbands heart stops, we the medical staff would not try and resuscitate him. Essentially at that point he would..."

With anger and resentment, Jason responds, "YEAH, WE GET IT, DOCTOR!"

"If you'll excuse me, I'll give you some privacy," the surgeon awkwardly responds as he walks out of his office.

Two Days Later

Ellen, Jason, Adam, and Jared, are standing around the gravesite. Larry's wooden coffin is slowly being lowered into the ground.

"I think we should get Mom out of here and back to the car," Adam whispers to Jason.

"OK, can you go ahead and take her? I'll meet you all in a few minutes," Jason requests with sorrow in his voice.

"Yeah, sure. Mom, let's get going," Adam directs wiping the tears from his eyes.

Adam and Jared struggle to escort Ellen away from the gravesite. Jason is there all alone with the back drop of a windy overcast sky. The smell of rain fills the air.

Kneeling, with tears in his eyes, Jason looks down at the coffin and attempts to speak out loud.

"Hey, Dad. I already miss you so much. I just wanted you to know, that I'm the man I am today because of you. I mean that! I've been thinking a lot over the last couple of days. I know if there

146

was one thing I could do to make you proud, it would be to make peace with Eric and be the older brother I never was to him growing up. It's time for me to do that. He needs me. And, Dad… I really need him right now." Jason wipes the tears from his eyes. "I know all you ever wanted me to do was love him as much as he loved me. Like you always told me, friends come and go, but my brothers will stand by my side, forever." Jason's voice begins to whimper. "I know now, you just didn't want me to make the same mistakes you did and I will always love you for that. Thank you for being the best dad I could ever ask for. I promise I will make you proud, always. Goodbye, Daddy! I love you, forever."

Toad pauses, stares up at the sky, and shouts out with a smile, "JAAASSSOOON!! JAAASSSOOON!!"

Losing my father broke my spirit. There's no other way to say it. Even though we didn't see eye-to-eye on many things, later in life I always looked up to him for the father he was. Sure, he embarrassed the shit out of me at times, but you know what... It made him who he was, my dad. I can look back now and love him for that. As I grew up, I learned to appreciate the way he tried to teach me about life and responsibility. It wasn't so much what he said, but more for what he did. When I became a father, I quickly learned that being a parent is the most difficult job in the world, if you do it the right way. (*laughing*) Listen, everyone makes mistakes and wishes they could hit the rewind button, but in the end you just gotta believe, most people do the best they can within their own set of circumstances. I know my father did.

(*Taking a short pause while wiping away tears*)

Grieving the loss of someone who is still alive, might be one of the most difficult challenges a person can face in life. We knew my brother Eric was struggling with his mental health. Even prior to his "official" diagnosis, he had shown signs that something wasn't right. During his teenage years, was when we began to see the first signs of his erratic and self-destructive behavior.

How could someone look so healthy on the outside, but be so sick on the inside? That was the question I struggled to answer for years.

Moving in and out of state hospitals eventually took its toll on Eric and my entire family. My brother became a shell of the person he was. The guilt that I had for the way I mistreated him growing up weighed heavy on me every day. I just wish I had listened to my father all those years.

148

Since I couldn't go back in time, I had only one option. To live in the moment and be the best brother I could be, for the rest of my life. That's what I will do!"

(Taking another pause)

Losing my childhood best friend was devastating. Not only the way I found out, but because I never had any idea Jimmy was struggling the way he was. Like my brother Eric, sometimes the people that appear the happiest on the outside, are the ones tormented the most on the inside.

It took me years, to fully process what had happen to my blood brother. We had stayed in touch over time, through letters and emails. Everything seemed fine. We had even talked about meeting up several times, but unfortunately it just never ended up happening. I had always thought, if only I had just gotten in my car, could I have done something that may have prevented this horrific tragedy from occurring?

(Taking a deep breath and slowly exhales)

The years after leaving Mayfair Court continued to have its ups and downs. Moving away was very difficult to deal with. It took me a long time to come to terms with my reality. It was my safe place. The perfect snapshot of what life should and could be. However, as time went on, I began to realize that no situation is perfect forever. Heartache and challenges, will find you wherever you live and whatever age you are. What matters the most, is how you deal with those obstacles once they arrive. How do you keep pushing forward? How do we lean on the ones we love for strength? How do we find the grit to keep fighting out of the corners and not go down?

For me, that day had come. It was time to go back, time to face the pain, and most importantly relive all the joy. I didn't know what to expect, but I was finally ready to go home.

Chapter Fifteen
Back to Where It All Began

Mayfair Court
The Summer of 2018

J ason is driving his car with his wife Andrea and two children. Rachel, age ten and Andrew, age eight are in the back seat as they're rapidly approaching Mayfair Court.

"Dad, I can't believe we're finally here! I'm so excited to see where you grew up. I've heard about this place my entire life. It's so weird, I'm almost kind of nervous!" Rachel blurts out.

"You're nervous? I haven't been back here in thirty years!" Jason chuckles.

The Shapiros approach their destination. Everyone is filled with immense anticipation as the car slowly makes a left turn onto Jason's childhood street.

"Dad, I see the Mayfair Court street sign!" Rachel shouts out with excitement.

"WOW! I can't believe it, guys! Everything looks exactly how I remember it!" Jason expresses in amazement.

"What was your address again, Daddy?" Andrew questions with curiosity.

Proudly, Jason confirms, "6629, it's the blue house with bricks on the front."

Jason slowly drives down the street in awe as he proceeds to give an emotional tour.

"Hey, that's where the Thompson's lived... And over there is where we would set up our skateboard ramps. We would jump off those things for hours! I'm sure we drove everyone on the block crazy. That was Bobby's house over on the right, the one with the brown stones on the front. Did I ever tell you about his snort-laugh?" Jason chuckles.

"DAD! DAD! I found it! There's your house! Go knock on the door!" Rachel yells out with pure elation.

"OH MY GOD! There it is! WOW! She's held up really well after all these years... Exactly how I remember. Guys, see that giant oak tree in the middle of the front yard? It was the size of a bush when we moved in. Now it's gotta be over thirty feet tall! I just can't believe it!" Jason explains with excitement.

The car pulls over to the side of the street and parks. Emotions rapidly begin to rush through Jason's mind as he begins to profusely sweat.

With concern, Andrea questions, "Are you OK, honey?"

Dazed, Jason softly replies, "Yeah, I'm OK," as he stares intently at his childhood home.

Suddenly, time stands still. Jason vividly flashes back, to the last time he saw Jimmy and said goodbye to him.

"Listen Jay, I wrote you a letter."

"Wait, you wrote me a letter?" Jason questions with laughter.

"Yeah, I wrote a letter, dude. I was going to give it to you before you left today, but I decided to leave it in the tree-mouth. It will be waiting for you. So, you better come back to visit very soon, 'cause it took me forever to write it!" Both boys laugh.

With absolute certainty, Jason confirms, "I'll be back. I don't know when, but I will be and I promise I will read it."

The emotional memory abruptly fades away.

"Dad, are you OK? We were all calling your name and you didn't say anything. You're just like, staring into space," Andrew confirms.

"He's ALWAYS staring into space!" Rachel responds laughing.

Jason quietly mumbles, "I'm alright... I'm alright."

Drawn by the intense flashback, Jason quickly puts the car in drive and adamantly proceeds down the street toward Jimmy's childhood home.

"Where the heck is he going?" Andrew questions.

With no response, Jason continues driving and pulls up in front of Jimmy's house. He puts the car in park.

Annoyed, Rachel questions, "Dad, what are you doing?"

Andrea finally answers, "I don't know what he's doing, but just sit back and be patient. PLEASE!"

Without warning, Jason calmly gets out of the car with the engine running. He begins to cautiously walk up the side of Jimmy's yard. The neighbor's dog begins aggressively barking through a screened in patio. Nervous, Jason pushes forward and steadily continues. As he gets closer, the gigantic tree branches towering high above Jimmy's childhood house can be seen. Jason walks around the corner and stops short in absolute amazement. He stares at the magnificence, of what the tree has now become. The sunlight shoots through the enormous leaves as the massive branches steadily sway in the wind.

"Wow, just incredible," Jason mumbles as he feels the intense aura radiating from the tree.

The weathered and rotted remains of the tree house are still intact, just as Jason remembered from thirty years prior.

With emotions pulsing throughout his entire body, Jason bravely steps closer to the tree and pauses. Suddenly, he reaches deep into the tree-mouth. He begins to pull out handfuls of damp leaves and franticly tosses them to the ground. Unexpectedly, a large slimy frog jumps out and startles him. Nervously, he pauses, takes a deep breath, and continues to pull out clumps of tree debris.

After several minutes of searching, nothing is found. Frustrated, Jason decides to give up. Defeated, he begins to walk away, with a look of utter disappointment.

Without warning, a soothing cool breeze flows through the humid hot summer air. Just like when Jason and Jimmy would sit in the tree house many years ago. Something inside his body pushes him to turn around.

He intently walks back toward the tree-mouth and with conviction Jason reaches as deep as he can into the tree. FINALLY! He feels something! With his eyes closed and heart pounding through his chest, Jason begins to steadily pull out a plastic Ziploc bag. It's completely covered with dirt, moss, and wet leaves. He immediately attempts to wipe off the bag with his hands and then hold it up to the sunlight. Through the plastic, Jason can see the remnants of something neatly folded up. He carefully unseals the bag with uncontrolled curiosity. He slowly pulls out what appears to be the letter Jimmy had written thirty years ago. The paper is yellowed and the writing has faded. Jason fumbles to frantically unfold and read the letter.

JIMMY'S 15-YEAR-OLD VOICE NARRATES

Jay,   July 6, 1989

It's the night before you move away. I can't sleep, so I decided
  to go up into the treehouse and write you this letter.
You know when I'm stressed out and sad, I always feel better
  when I'm up here. There are a few things on my mind that
  for some reason I felt like I needed to tell you.
The first thing is about your dad. I know he can embarrass
  you and drive you crazy sometimes. Hell, my dad does the
  same to me, but he loves you a lot, Jay. I see it in his eyes
  when he talks to you. He just wants the best for you and
  all of your brothers. You're really lucky to have him as your father.
  I hope you forgive him for anything he has done to upset you.
The next thing is really important! Please take care of your brother, Eric.
He's a good kid and he looks up to you more then
  you will ever know. Always look out for him, because
I know he would do the same for you.
The last thing, I don't know what's going to happen
  in my life, but I want you to always follow your dreams, Jay.
You can do anything you set your mind to, so never ever give up, ever!
Even though we won't be seeing each other much anymore,
I will always be with you, cheering you on
Our memories will live forever!

                                        Love you like a brother,
                                        Your BEST friend!
                                              Jimmy

"DADDY! Are you OK?" Rachel yells out as she walks up behind Jason, holding her great-grandfather's camera.

Startled, Jason responds, "Oh, I didn't see you there. I'm OK, baby."

"Can we please go? We're getting tired of sitting in the car," Rachel pleads with annoyance.

"Go ahead and tell Mommy I will be right there," Jason informs as he puts the treasured letter in his pocket.

"OK, Daddy," Rachel responds as she darts away.

Jason intently looks up at the tree one last time as the wind blows through the branches. He smiles, kisses the tree, and projects out loud, "I love you too, Jimmy... I love you too."

He walks back to the car and gets in.

"Are you OK?!" Andrea questions with immense concern.

Now, finally at peace, Jason responds with a smile, "I'm OK, babe, I'm OK," as he tenderly kisses Andrea on the forehead.

"Alright guys, I think I'm ready to go knock on that door now!" Jason announces with a slow deep breath.

"YAY!" both kids yell out in unison.

Jason responds, "I just hope whoever lives there doesn't chase me away with a broom!" Everyone laughs.

"Daddy, do you think your playground is still set up in your backyard?" Andrew questions with excitement.

"Dad, what about the rock you and your brothers would jump off of. I wonder if that's still there," Rachel ponders.

"I don't know, but let's go find out!" Jason responds as he smiles at Andrea.

He drives the car back up the street and proceeds to park in front of his childhood home.

"Hey, kids, Daddy has to do this by himself," Andrea explains with empathy.

"OK, everyone, wish me luck," Jason responds as he opens the car door and hesitantly gets out.

Apprehensive, he begins to steadily walk up his childhood driveway. Memories of years ago begin to flood his mind.

Jason walks over and cautiously opens the screen door. He slowly closes his eyes and takes a gasping breath. Boiling with anxiety, he knocks on the front door.

After waiting for several excruciating minutes, no one answers. Just as Jason steps away, the door cracks open, and reveals a young boy standing in the entryway. He resembles how Jason looked as a child.

"Hi, are your parents home?" Jason nervously questions.

"Yes," the boy responds.

The two stare at each other as if they had an unexplainable connection.

"James, honey, you know you're not supposed to open the door. I'm sorry, can I help you?" the young mother questions in a friendly tone as she stands behind the boy.

Shocked and dazed, Jason softly mumbles, "Did you just call him James? Umm, I'm sorry. Hi, my name is Jason Shapiro. I really do apologize for bothering you."

"Hey, Dad!" both of Jason's children shout as they casually walk up behind him.

"Guys, come on. I told you to stay in the car," Jason whispers as the young mother giggles.

"I know this sounds absolutely crazy, but um... this is the house I actually grew up in," Jason anxiously explains.

"WOW! No way! Really? How cool is that?" the mother responds with a warm smile.

Jason proudly informs, "Yeah, we moved into this house back in the summer of 1983."

"My dad's an old man!" Andrew announces with laughter.

Curious, the mother responds, "So how old were you when you moved into this house?"

"Well, I was eight," Jason replies with a grin.

"Wow, like you, James. So… did you like growing up on this street? Do you have any fun stories from the good ole days?" the mother questions with curiosity.

Jason makes eye contact with both of his children as they smile at their father with happiness.

"Well… As a matter of fact, I do!" Jason chuckles and responds with pure contentment.

In unison, Rachel and Andrew put their hands on their head and grumble, "We're gonna be here for a while!"

After several long minutes of spirited conversation with the mother, Jason walks down his childhood driveway for the last time. He's holding Andrew and Rachel's hands as intense emotions continue to flow throughout his entire body.

Without warning, James darts out of the garage past Jason holding a water gun. He begins chasing a group of young girls down the street. They creatively dodge the water, desperately trying not to get wet. The echoing sound of childhood joy and laughter fills the air. Unexpectedly, one of the girls spins around and pegs James with a water balloon in the stomach.

"Wow! I always wondered how that ended," Jason announces while chuckling.

Looking up, Jason stares deep into the piercing blue sky. Tears of infinite happiness well in his eyes. He then watches as the next generation of children on Mayfair Court create their own magical memories that they will one day cherish.

Every house has a secret and every street has a story. For some reason that's what kept running through my mind that day. There was such an important part of my life hidden within the walls of that house and in the branches of that tree. It was fascinating to think that the memories of my past could only be seen if you knew my story. There was actually something comforting and special about that.

Going back to a place where we experienced joy with someone who has passed away is heartbreaking. There's no other way to say it. For me, I had no other option but to go. I had an opened wound and it could only be healed by returning home.

Finally, I was ready to leave my past behind. I knew it was safe and would always be waiting for me if I ever came back.

Before I could fully be at peace, there was one more important part of my life that I needed to repair. Something that I had been struggling with for decades. Something that I knew even at a young age, I would have to face one day.

Chapter Sixteen

Making Amends with Regret

Current Day
South Florida State Mental Hospital

S ir, visiting hours end in ten minutes," the nurse politely reminds as she unlocks the cold steel door and walks in the room.

"Oh, sure, no problem," Jason replies as he slowly closes his tattered scrapbook.

The cover was drawn by hand and is titled: THE MAGIC OF MAYFAIR.

There's a heavier set bald man sitting close to Jason at the table, dressed in stained grey sweats and navy Velcro sneakers.

In a medicated, emotionless, voice, he says, "Thank you so much for telling me all the stories again."

"It's not easy for me, pal, but I enjoy doing it," Jason replies with a smile.

"Jason, can I get one more snack before you leave?" requests the man.

"Yeah, sure, what do you want?" questions Jason.

"I'll take a bag of potato chips, please," the man graciously responds.

Jason takes his wallet out of his back pocket, removes a dollar and leaves it opened on the table.

A small piece of paper in the clear slot with his driver's license can be seen. It reads, *"There's no buddy like a brother"*.

Jason returns from the vending machine with the potato chips and hands them to the man.

"Well, I guess it's time for me to get going," Jason mentions as he slides his wallet back into his pocket.

The man looks Jason in the eye with a blank stare and responds, "Thank you very much for coming to visit me. I look forward to it every week."

The two lovingly embrace as Jason firmly pats the man's back.

"Listen, it was great seeing you. Please take care of yourself. Oh, and make sure you're taking your medication… And eating enough," requests Jason as he quickly wipes the tears from his eyes.

"I will. All I do is eat," the man responds in a serious tone as Jason chuckles and smiles.

After another emotional embrace, Jason replies, "I'll see you next week, OK?"

"I love you, Toad," the man replies with a medicated laugh.

"I love you most, Berry," Jason responds with a smile.

Jason walks toward the exit. He pauses, turns around, and waves goodbye as he leaves.

"OK, Eric, time to go!" the nurse directs with a smile.

Jason walks out of the doors and is soon no longer in sight.

"You know, I have to tell you something, Eric. Whoever that man is, he must love you A LOT! He's here every single week, with that same beat up looking scrapbook, telling you the same ole stories," the nurse compliments with warm laughter.

"Oh, that's my big brother, Jason. I ask him to bring that scrapbook with him. I love listening to all his childhood memories, especially when he went back to visit our old house. It makes me really happy. You know... We didn't always get along growing up, but we do now. That's all that matters," Eric responds for the first time with joy in his eyes.

"Well Eric, I have a feeling he would do just about anything for you... And whatever is in that scrapbook he reads to you, it must be pretty darn special," the nurse replies with confidence.

Emotional, Eric finally smiles and agrees, "It is very special... It is very special!"

A single tear of happiness trickles down Eric's face.

The End

PHOTO ALBUM

THE PEOPLE BEHIND
THE MAGIC

I always felt this picture cap-
tured how proud my father
was of his family. It still hangs
in my mother's house today.

Here's a good shot of my mush-
room shaped hair and tube socks
pulled up to my thighs. Deep
down, there was always a part of
me that loved my brother Eric.

Here's my Uncle Richie and his magical
mustache in 1987. I would love to see him
try and reenact this photo today!

Going to Toys "R" US with my Aunt Frances was always a treat. I loved roaming the aisles of never-ending happiness.

I was obsessed with The Karate Kid and thought I could possibly win the All Valley Karate Championship!

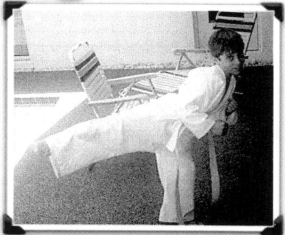

Looking back at photos of Eric as a child still triggers regret and pain so many years later.

This is the youngest Shapiro brother, Herm. My father had a nickname for everyone. Even his own children couldn't avoid getting one assigned to them.

Here is my father in action at a retail trade show in the late 80's. He loved working hard and being productive. I'm very fortunate that his work ethic was passed down to my brothers and me.

My Uncle Steven (my mother's brother) has always encouraged me to dream big and never give up. He has been one of the biggest supporters of me writing this book.

Here is Bub after my dad encouraged him to wear this crazy concoction. Look how sweet that Chattahoochee patio deck looked in the background!

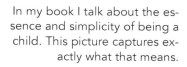

When my father wasn't reprimanding my Uncle Richie for tearing his patio screen door, he could actually be a loving older brother.

In my book I talk about the essence and simplicity of being a child. This picture captures exactly what that means.

THE MAN IN WHITE, Max Shapiro with my Nanny Rhoda. If you're from South Florida and you're my age, chances are your grandparents lived in Wynmoore! I miss them both very much.

My Nanny Gloria and Poppy Al. Unfortunately, he passed away 3 months after this photo was taken. My Grandma is 91 years young today and hasn't missed a beat since the day we sang the song *Gloria* to her.

My birthday party salute with members of the Mayfair Court Crew. Back in the 1980's, you had a pool party if you lived in Florida. Eric is in the front. He just wanted to be part of whatever I was doing.

Jason T. Shapiro

My father's Sunday morning ritual was reading the TV guide. He loved the thrill of shouting out what movies were going to be on.

This is one of my favorite pictures. It captures everything that was special about growing up on Mayfair Court.

Our pool seemed like the size of the ocean and our backyard was definitely the size of a football field. When you're a kid, everything seems bigger than life.

171

I kept this picture of Eric in my wallet for years. It was taken a few months before his battle with Paranoid Schizophrenia began. He had just left for college and was so excited for his future.

My father would always make us do these cheesy poses for the camera. Eric was home from college. He was struggling with his illness but was still able to graduate. It showed what a fighter he was.

This photo was taken at Nanny Rhoda's house. Despite the horrible side effects of the medication he was taking, Eric never stopped smiling.

Unfortunately, as the years went on, there were many pictures like this one. Eric wasn't able to go to any of our weddings or be there for the birth of our children. I get emotional just thinking about it.

I met my beautiful wife Andrea in 2005. She always has cared deeply for Eric, despite only seeing him a few times since we met.

I wanted my best friend standing next to me the day of my Bar Mitzvah. I think of him every day. I have felt his presence many times while writing this book.

The year after this picture was taken, my father lost his job. Sitting home day after day broke his spirit. He slowly started to deteriorate, physically and mentally.

My amazing family! They have been by my side during the entire journey of writing this book. thank them for understanding how important telling this story for me.

My mission from the first sentence I wrote is to make this story into a movie one day. My daughter shares that vision. Here is the movie poster she made. The premiere is less than two years away. I better get moving!

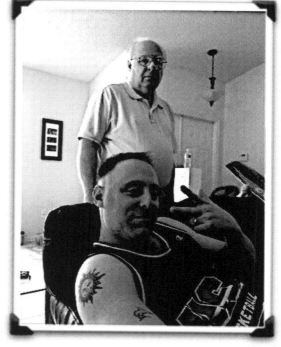

This is the last picture ever taken of my father. It was the day before the car accident. Health issues and my brother's mental illness had taken a toll on him. He was a shell of the man I knew. I am so thankful GOD gave me this last day with him.

Dedication

This story is dedicated to Lawrence Peter Shapiro, Eric Bryon Shapiro, and William John Gange Jr.; three of the most beautiful souls, whose stories will now live on forever...

Made in the USA
Monee, IL
05 March 2020